MW00780361

THE
MARKETING BLUEPRINT

"As construction professionals, we put a lot of focus on production and the quality of our finished product. What we tend to leave to fate, though, is how those projects come to us in the first place. Spencer Powell knows the formula for this part of the equation, and he lays it out clearly in this book!"

—**Spencer Padgett**, Builder-in-Residence, CoConstruct

"Spencer Powell is a guru in the world of digital marketing. Since digital is the wave of the future, that's an essential skill! In this book, he leads us through the very specific process of creating strategies and tactics to drive leads through the roof. If you're managing your company's digital marketing push, you've gotta get this book!"

—**Victoria Downing**, President, Remodelers Advantage Inc.

"If you're a remodeler who wants to create a web presence to draw in traffic that converts to quality project leads—there's no one I'd more highly recommend than Spencer Powell. Read this book and—most importantly—implement what it has to say."

—**Kyle Hunt**, RemodelYourMarketing.com

"Whether you're just starting out with your online marketing, or you need to refine and fix what's not working, you need to read this book. Just do what Spencer says. Not only does he give you the nuts and bolts of how it all works, but also he's a practitioner and an expert in helping construction businesses grow their businesses with the methods described in this book."

—**Shawn Van Dyke**, Author of *Profit First for Contractors*

"The Remodelers Marketing Blueprint is a must-read for any professional remodeler or custom home builder looking to take their marketing efforts to the next level. Spencer's done a marvelous job of laying this out perfectly and explaining complex concepts in everyday language, making it very actionable to implement the steps. The wisdom contained inside these pages is unparalleled for our industry!"

—**Bryan Kaplan**, Founder of Construction Consulting

"This book could just have easily been called *A Remodeler's Guide to Digital Marketing*. In it, Spencer covers everything you need to know about social media, websites, content marketing and more. If you're in the dark when it comes to getting found online, then this book is for you."

—**Mark Harari**, Author of *Lobster on a Cheese Plate: How to Stand Out, Attract the Best Clients, and Win Every Sale that Comes Your Way*

The
REMODELER MARKETING BLUEPRINT

How to Attract Quality Leads, Increase Sales, and Dominate Your Competition

SPENCER POWELL

RIVER GROVE
BOOKS

Published by River Grove Books
Austin, TX
www.rivergrovebooks.com

Distributed by River Grove Books

Design and composition by Greenleaf Book Group
Cover design by Greenleaf Book Group
Cover Images: Texture of wood background close up; construction
blueprints in rolls isolated 3d render; Illustration for drawing vector,
used under license from Shutterstock.com

Publisher's Cataloging-in-Publication data is available.

Print ISBN: 978-1-63299-339-7

eBook ISBN: 978-1-63299-340-3

First Edition

CONTENTS

Preface

When I first got started in marketing, I didn't know anything about it. However, I did know what I didn't like—ads. I didn't like seeing commercials for stuff I didn't want or need. When I turned on the radio, I didn't like waiting to get back to the music. As I surfed the internet, I didn't like having to close pop-ups.

The ads were annoying and interrupted what I was trying to do. I didn't realize it at the time, but I was looking for a better way to do marketing. Was it possible to create marketing that people actually liked? As I continued to dive into the world of websites, social media, blogging, search engine optimization, and all things digital, I realized that maybe it was really possible.

I started writing blog posts, answering questions people had about digital marketing. Soon people started finding my blog and leaving comments about how helpful it was. Then they started reaching out to me for help.

Ah-ha! Creating helpful, educational, and entertaining information pulls people toward you. Most of those people didn't actually want to do the work, so they reached out and hired me. This was the start of a journey that has transformed the way I think about marketing and changed my life. Over the next ten years, I continued to put education at the forefront of the marketing I was doing for my company, Builder Funnel, as well as for our clients, remodeling companies.

Educate, entertain, and inform, and you'll become a thought leader and drive your business forward.

As you read through this book, I want you to keep an open mind. Some of the sections may seem like they don't apply to you or your business, and at times you may think I'm a little bit crazy. But everything I'm going to share with you I've been implementing for over a decade, and these strategies have driven millions in sales for my own company and over $100 million in sales for my clients. The internet is a powerful tool, and I want to show you how to adapt your marketing. The internet is definitely not going away; it's only going to become more and more integrated into our lives.

Keep your mind open. Look at the strategies, stories, and examples I share with you and think about how you might apply them in your business.

Let's start creating better marketing. Let's create marketing people actually enjoy.

Acknowledgments

As it turns out, writing a book is really tough. For me, it was made easier by the help and support of so many individuals whom I'd like to thank.

I would have never completed this book if it weren't for the love and support from my wife Rachael. She encouraged me to get up all those early mornings to write before the sun came up. She urged me to keep going when I hit lulls, and she never doubted me for a second even when I doubted myself.

I'd like to thank my parents, Wes and Karen. Not once have they ever told me that something wasn't possible. They never tried to limit me. People who have big goals and dreams often get discouraged early by the people closest to them. Influential people in our lives, like parents, can unwittingly discourage their children because they don't want to see them fail. They recommend you don't start because the idea is too big or too crazy. I'm grateful to my parents for never discouraging me because they didn't want to see me fail. This has allowed me to view life, my goals, and my dreams without limitation.

Thank you to my brother Blake. By writing his own book, he was the one who planted the seed that I could even start this journey. Without him sharing details about his own book writing journey and the strategies he was using, I never would have even started.

Thank you to my sister Casey who was an ever-present encouraging voice for me on this project. She cheered me on and was always impressed with the progress I was making even if I didn't feel like I was getting anywhere. Her positivity shined through on those tough days.

To the family members who always support me, get excited about what I'm up to, and encourage me to keep going: Tim, Kim, Whitney, Jerome, Hannah, Lily, and Brooks.

To everyone on the Builder Funnel team who supported me on this journey, thank you for being a part of our amazing company and showing up every day for our clients to help them grow their businesses. Thank you for your support, inspiration and encouragement: Danielle Russell, Steven Fielding, Taylor Rennick, Danielle Fauteaux, Nicole Raymond, Malachi Price, Cody Van Hooser, Ashley Covella, Chris Root, Kelly McNamara, Mari Carballo, Tyler Sinden, Drew Wagner, Andi Paradis, Chase Urquhart, Samsodin Dianalan Tantua, Jeff Hodges, and Ruth Gardner.

To all those who have been a part of my getting there—a group of men that I've known since we were boys. You guys push me to reach higher, be better, and have fun along the way: John, Clayton, Tim, Chris, Jesse, Nathan, Eli, and Cal.

To individuals in the industry who have become cheerleaders and friends: Shawn Van Dyke, Bryan Kaplan, David Supple,

Jim Walker, Will Giesey, Andrew Giannattasio, Kyle Hunt, Mark Harari, Victoria Downing, and Spencer Padgett.

To the entire Greenleaf Publishing team: Lindsay Bohls for keeping everything on track and on schedule, Jay Hodges for making my writing more clear and direct, Neil Gonzalez for his creative process and expertise in design, and Jessica Reyes for helping me get to the finish line with a product I'm incredibly proud of.

Finally, to my two boys Carter and Teddy. Your lives are just beginning, and you've already pushed me to be a better man.

CHAPTER 1

The Script Has Flipped

THE WAY CONSUMERS SHOP HAS CHANGED. HAS YOUR MARKETING?

The way we shop and buy things today looks extremely different than it did in the early-to-mid-2000s. Think about how you used to buy a new TV. You may have been exposed to the idea through a commercial. After seeing the commercial, you thought, "Man, I really need that new sixty-inch HDTV." Then you went to the store and talked to a sales rep.

The salesperson had all the control and all the information. If you wanted to know the specs on something and how it compared to other brands or models, you'd rely on that individual for the information to make your decision.

The script has flipped. Salespeople have almost no power, and the consumer has taken it all. If you want to research TVs, you go to Google or Amazon or YouTube and look for information.

Reviews, ratings, tutorials, comparisons, specs, pricing, and anything else you could possibly want to know is now online. You can do all the research on your own, and you never have to talk to a salesperson.

In our world of remodeling, we're not quite to that point (although we may get there), but we're still seeing this major shift influence the way we need to approach our marketing. The consumer still has all the power. If they want to know the cost of a kitchen remodel or how long it will take, they go to Google. If they want to compare companies, they go to Google. If they want to see design trends, examples of work, and even read reviews or watch testimonials, they go online.

You need to match your marketing process to the way people shop and buy. This means meeting the consumer where they are in their research process. It means creating the type of information they are looking for and making it available on your website and social media channels. It's not good enough to post pretty pictures on your website anymore. You have to create helpful, educational content. You have to think of yourself as a thought leader. (You are!)

Your prospects and customers don't know anything about what you do. Well, they know a little bit, but it's probably 1–3 percent of what you know. Because we're in it every day, the industry and what we do feel like common knowledge. But talk to a friend for ten minutes about your typical workday, and you'll quickly discover they don't know any of the specifics about what you do. Why would they? They aren't in our industry!

Your basic knowledge can be expert knowledge to your prospects and customers. By sharing basic information like how the remodeling process works, what the latest design trends are, how much it will cost, and how long it will take, you start to position yourself as a thought leader.

In this book, I'm going to show you how to separate yourself from your competitors by sharing information that you already know on the internet. Sounds easy, right? It is easy in theory, but in my experience, almost no one is willing to follow through on the execution. However, it's my hope that after reading this book, you'll be one of the few who *do* follow through, and you'll start to become the go-to expert in your service area.

I've been implementing this strategy of thought leadership content online for over a decade. Over that time, I've literally built my company from nothing. I had no connections, no experience, and no money to invest. But I had time. I learned about digital marketing and shared what I learned through my website, blog, and then later webinars, videos, and podcasts.

The more I shared, the more people found me. The more people found me, the more opportunities I created for myself. Now, my company, Builder Funnel, is a team of fourteen full-time marketers, and we've helped our remodeling clients close projects totaling over $100 million, all by creating content online.

We live in an amazing time. You don't have to have the biggest budget anymore. You don't have to be the biggest or the best company anymore. You just have to be the most helpful.

I'm going to walk you through the process of becoming a thought leader step-by-step. By the end of the book, you'll have a blueprint for establishing yourself and your company as a thought leader. And don't worry—this isn't some pie-in-the-sky idea. I'll connect the dots with digital tactics like blogging, SEO, email, social media, and your website so that you'll see how this content generates real leads and real sales.

The process of becoming a thought leader will actually provide your business with stability because it will help you build a more predictable lead pipeline so that you can weather the storms (recessions) and stay strong during the slow seasons throughout the year.

Are you ready to become a thought leader? Let's get started.

CHAPTER 2

How to Think About Your Website

What if you had a salesperson who never took breaks, didn't take holidays, never needed to eat or sleep, and always delivered your message the same way to every prospect? Wouldn't that be incredible? That person can exist in the form of your website. If you build a powerful website, it will actually do the marketing, prospecting, and even—partially or completely—closing deals for you. Someone isn't going to buy a kitchen remodel and pay for it online like she buys stuff on Amazon (although we might get there!), but your website can bring her 90 percent of the way to the close.

I want you to imagine a world where you have prospects calling your company or filling out your contact form to discuss a project. These prospects have already learned about you and your company. They understand your process and the types of projects you work on. They also have a good sense of what pricing will look like and how long it will take. By the time they've made it to an initial phone call, they are well educated and haven't opted out. They are a good fit for you. They are the ideal client.

This is all possible because you have something extremely powerful (and often massively underutilized) at your disposal: your website. Yes, your website can make this happen.

Your website should be the center of all your marketing activities. I don't know why we get it in our heads that people don't research big purchases like remodels or custom homes online. We search for cars, houses, hot tubs, and jewelry online. We'll even make purchases in the thousands if not tens of thousands of dollars without even talking to a sales professional. So you can be sure that people are looking for information online about remodeling their home.

Your website should be the hub of all information for the consumer. It can house the following:

- Blog posts
- Project photos
- Team and company information
- Your remodeling process
- Videos
- And more

Your website is kind of like a digital showroom on steroids. You're not limited to a set amount of information. You can display as many projects as you want. You can showcase videos that tell your company story and how your process works and let people hear from happy clients via testimonials.

The best part about having a digital showroom that lives online? It's open 24/7, and people can access it from their couch or bed on their iPad. We live in a world where the consumer wants convenience. We want things now. By maintaining a robust website, you give your consumers the ability to learn more about you and your company by investing minimal time.

Think about the way you do research. You want to learn everything you can about what you're buying and, for larger purchases, who you're buying from. Your website should provide all the necessary information your prospect is looking for.

Take a look at your website. It should provide answers to common questions your prospects have, such as:

- How long does it take to remodel?
- What are the current design trends?
- How much will this cost?
- What does the remodeling process look like?
- What if I don't know what design or look and feel I want?
- Can I stay in my home while the remodel takes place?

Does your website provide answers to these common questions? Does it showcase your past projects? If you said no to these questions, this is a great time to start rethinking the purpose of your website. Your website is your #1 marketing tool and salesperson (if you build it the right way). And this salesperson sells the exact same way every time and never takes days off—even for holidays!

All this being said, a website is not an "if you build it, they will come" sort of endeavor. It needs fuel. It needs content. I'll be going into content creation in much more detail later.

For now, just know that your website has two major components to it:

- The design (the look and feel of it)
- The performance (how many prospects are actually visiting and how many are converting into leads)

Most web design companies want to sell you a new design because that's where they are strong, and that's their business model. That's how they make money. And they've gotten really good at explaining why you always seem to need a new design.

However, most of the time, you don't need a new design. You need more performance. In the chapters to come, I'll show you how to improve your website performance even if your design isn't top-of-the-line yet. You can start increasing the number of prospects who visit your website right away even before you start working on a brand-new design.

And that's where content comes into play. In today's internet world, content is the foundation of all your success. You must have great content to thrive.

CHAPTER 3

Create Content That Matters to Your Customer

Before we talk about content, we need to know your customer. Is she married? Single? Does she have kids? Do she and her partner both work? What are her hobbies? Where does she shop? What are her goals, fears, dreams, and challenges?

In marketing, we call your ideal client a marketing persona. Your persona is a fictional character that represents the client you want to attract and work with on a regular basis. The more specifically you describe your persona and the more details you can put down, the better your marketing efforts will be. You want to get to a point where you're truly speaking your persona's language. You're using her exact words and phrases. When she reads your marketing messages, it should feel like you're in her head, thinking what she's thinking.

This allows you to connect on a deeper level with your persona. Before you start creating content, it's critical that you at least have an outline of your persona so that you know who you're writing to. The more specific you can get, the better. Why do you think this book is written specifically for remodelers? It's because I wanted to provide super-specific examples that are extremely relevant. That way, you get more value, and you know that I understand your world. It's the same with your customers. They should feel like you get them.

HOMEWORK: BUILD YOUR MARKETING PERSONA

I've supplied a persona template that can be found on my company website: builderfunnel.com. If you're like me, you probably don't want to stop the flow of reading to work on the activity. If you want to keep powering through, I've also included a section at the back of the book that summarizes all the homework steps in order so that you can get the most out of the book after you complete it.

CHAPTER 4

Marketing Lingo

Before we get too far, I want to quickly review some marketing lingo. As a full-time digital marketer, I use these terms on a daily basis, but I know you probably don't. I want to make sure we're on the same page so that you can get the most out of the book.

We've already covered "content" and "marketing persona." Here are the other terms you need to get familiar with:

- Website traffic (or traffic): The raw number of people visiting your website. If you look at your website analytics tool (such as Google Analytics), you can find this number.

- Organic traffic: The number of people visiting your website from search engines like Google or Bing.

Increasing organic traffic is a good indicator that your website is ranking and being found when people search online.

- Website conversion rate (or conversion rate): The way we calculate conversion rate is by taking the number of website form submissions, dividing it by your total website traffic, and then multiplying by 100 to get your percentage. Example: 10 form submissions divided by 1,000 visitors x 100 = 1 percent conversion rate.

- Lead: Someone who fills out a form on your website.

- Marketing qualified lead: Someone who has filled out a form on your website and also taken a specific set of actions (e.g., opened three or more marketing emails and visited the website on three separate occasions).

- Sales qualified lead: Someone who has talked to a salesperson who has deemed them a good fit. Ultimately, they might not become a customer, but they are qualified to be one, and you want to work with them.

- Inbound marketing: A technique for drawing customers to products and services via content.

CHAPTER 5

Build Your Marketing Funnel

I first learned about the power of marketing funnels when someone bought from me years after we first connected. I realized that every person I talked to wasn't necessarily ready to make a purchase. Some prospects were just discovering a problem or a desire they had. Some were in the dreaming phase. Others were pretty certain of what they wanted, but they needed more information. A small percentage were ready to move forward right away.

Rather than dismissing the dreamers or the people who just wanted to extract information from me, I decided to embrace them. If I could help them, they'd see me in a good light, and I would have a better chance of earning their business when they were actually ready to make a purchase.

Plus, it just felt like the right thing to do. These people all needed help in some way. They needed to learn about the process or the cost. They wanted to know what the right solution looked like for them. They wanted to know how everything worked.

This goes for your prospects too. Most of them haven't remodeled before. They don't know how long it's going to take, how much it will cost, who they should trust and hire, or what to expect.

You may be thinking that you don't have time to help all these people for free or that you can't afford to answer every single question that your prospects have. I'd argue that you can't afford not to. Plus, I'll show you some really cool ways to automate your helpfulness at a scale that will allow you to spend most of your time with the prospects who are closer to a buying decision while still adding value and earning trust with prospects who are maybe months or years away from being your next customer.

Enter the marketing funnel.

WHAT IS A MARKETING FUNNEL?

A funnel allows you to visualize your prospects' buyer journeys. A buyer journey is the path a prospect takes en route to making a decision and purchasing. Your prospects have superpowers, because they can defy gravity and move up and down the funnel at will. Prospects will take slightly different paths depending on their personality and buying behavior. That being said, each prospect will generally go through or interact with each phase of the marketing funnel: top, middle, and bottom. At the top of the funnel, your prospect is dreaming. She is imagining a world where she can entertain in that spacious kitchen or relax in her spa-like master bathroom. The project isn't quite a reality yet. Moving forward with the project isn't really on her radar. At this stage, she could be anywhere from six months to multiple years away from actually starting her project. She also might never move forward.

At the middle of the funnel, your prospect is starting to think about how to make her dream a reality. She's trying to logistically figure out how to accomplish her goal. She's looking for information around cost, timeline, and process, and she's even starting to research potential companies like yours. At this stage, we also know that she is a more serious buyer, and her timeline has shortened. This stage is critical for earning her trust. At the top of the funnel, it's easy to get lost in the shuffle of pretty pictures on Instagram, Pinterest, and Houzz, but at the middle of the funnel, you can stand out a bit more.

Finally, we reach the bottom of the funnel. This is where your prospect is ready to make a decision. She's researched everything she can, and she's ready to talk. She's calling your office or filling out a form on your website asking to meet with you. At this stage, she wants to ask more questions and get super specific about what the project scope, cost, and timeline will look like. You're familiar with this stage because these are most likely the current majority of your leads.

The key to winning in today's marketing landscape is to engage with your prospect at each stage. Provide them with information. Help them along their journey. Understand that you're never going to force someone to make a decision on your timeline. If you understand that, you can focus all your efforts on earning their trust. That way, when they are ready to decide, you're top of mind and their only choice.

BUILD THE FOUNDATION

Your website should be the center of all your marketing efforts today. Think of it as your marketing hub. In this section, I'm going to show you how to build a proper website for design and performance.

These are the main components of a rock-solid marketing website:

- Design
- Powerful content management system
- Responsive Design
- Content
- Search engine optimization
- Conversion

Let's walk through each component in detail.

DESIGN VS. PERFORMANCE

Design is different from performance. The design of your website is how it looks and feels: the colors, the fonts, the flow, the content, and the photography. The performance of the website is more metrics-driven. Performance is the number of people who visit the website every day, week, or month and how many leads it generates.

A common mistake remodelers make is thinking that a website redesign will solve their problems. Often this results in thousands of dollars (or more) and months of time wasted. At the end of the website redesign project, you're left with a new and hopefully better-looking website. However, the same number of people are visiting the website, and you're getting the same number of leads. The design itself doesn't make the website perform better.

It's often advantageous to work on performance first—or simultaneously with design—rather than going down the redesign path, blindly thinking it will get you to your goals.

With that being said, let's dive into the design and performance of your website.

DESIGN

Design is important. When your prospects visit your website, they are checking you out. They want to see if you're the type of company they want to work with. Everyone wants to work with a professional company that does great work, even if they don't have the proper budget. Your website should represent the quality of work that you do.

What does this mean? No grainy photos, please! Your website is often the first impression of your company for your prospects.

Don't skimp on it. If you're doing a good job with your marketing, your website will be reaching several hundred people each month at a minimum and thousands, if not tens of thousands at the higher end. If you knew ten thousand people would walk into your office or showroom, wouldn't you want to invest in making sure that experience represents your brand and gives a good first impression?

Your website should have a strong design. Design is subjective, so I'm not going to go into a ton of detail, but just know that it should represent your brand and display professionally. Your photography should be professional and high resolution. It should attract and impress your target customer. Ideally, it will even turn away customers who aren't a good fit.

POWERFUL CONTENT MANAGEMENT SYSTEM

A content management system (CMS) is a software application that can be used to manage the creation and modification of digital content. You've probably heard of some of today's common platforms such as WordPress, Squarespace, or Wix. You don't have to use one of these platforms. The important thing is to make sure your platform allows for someone who doesn't know coding, which is used in website development, to update it. If you can edit a Word document, you should be able to edit your website.

Today, the power is in your hands. The old web design model was this: A company would design your website and build it on their proprietary system. This meant that no one except that company could make updates or changes. This ensured that they would be able to charge you for hosting on the platform (typically a monthly fee ranging from $10/month to $100/month), but they could also charge you hourly anytime you wanted to make changes as simple as adding a new project to your portfolio or adding or removing a team member from your team page. Don't get caught in this trap today. You should have full control of your domain, your hosting, and your CMS.

Another thing website companies like to do is help you buy your domain. However, when they do this, they often retain control of it in their account. If you ever decide to part ways, you have to go through the hassle of getting them to transfer the domain to you. If they play nice, this process is only a minor pain, but if they are difficult, it will be a huge time suck.

One time, I was working with a client to take their website live on a new marketing platform, and we needed access to the domain in order to do this. The company that had control of the domain didn't respond to emails or phone calls for weeks. When I finally got a response, they started playing hardball and told me it would be $500 to release control of the domain. Because I know how the transfer process works, I knew this was a complete BS charge. At the end of the day, my client had to pay the $500 just to get out of the situation. I share this story in hopes that it saves you time and money. You should always have control over your domain, even if you need someone else to manage it.

The same goes for hosting. There are plenty of great website hosting companies out there. There's almost no reason to work with a local hosting company. This business has generally become commoditized, so I usually recommend going with one of the major players where you know you can get 24/7 customer support, so if your website goes down on the weekend, they can help you get it up and running again. Expect to pay $20–$50/month for solid hosting with daily backups.

You may be wondering why I'm going into this level of detail in what's supposed to be a marketing book. At this point, I've personally had one-on-one conversations with hundreds of remodeling companies. It's amazing to me how many terrible scenarios I've seen. I want this section to arm you with the information you need anytime you're going through the process of designing, building, redesigning, or moving your website and its content.

I've seen too many remodelers get taken advantage of because this isn't their day-to-day world. Website and SEO companies do a great job of making this all sound uber complex and mystical. Hopefully, I'm providing you with enough information so that you ask the right questions and get the foundation you need to build an effective digital marketing machine on top of this platform.

RESPONSIVE DESIGN

It's a no-brainer that today your website should be easily viewed on all devices. This means desktop, tablet, and phone. This is called responsive design. When your website is built to be responsive, it adjusts automatically to the screen size.

You may be wondering if you need a separate mobile website. The short answer is no. You need a responsive website. Having a separate website for mobile causes several problems. First, it isn't what Google recommends. They specifically say they prefer responsive websites.

Second, if you have a separate website, you have to update your content in two places. This is a nightmare and ends up being at least double the work, but sometimes more because you have to understand how to edit both platforms.

Third, a mobile site will often have less information or more simplified information than the main site. This is terrible for user experience. If someone finds you on their phone and later wants to learn more on the desktop, there might be different information or missing information.

The long and the short of it? Make sure your website is responsive.

CONTENT

Content is what fuels your website. It can be written, audio, or visual. It can be your home page, team page, or a blog post. It can also be your portfolio page or a client video testimonial. It can even be a podcast or recorded seminar.

Content is also the foundation for search engine optimization (SEO), which I'll talk about next.

I want you to think about your last day or two. How often did you go to Google or ask your voice assistant (e.g., Google Home or Alexa) a question? If you're like me, it was several times. Because we have access to information literally in our pockets at all times, we take advantage of it. Talking about the football game and wondering where a player went to college? Google. Cooking or baking in the kitchen and need to know how many teaspoons in a tablespoon? Google. Heard a new word your teenaged kid used and have no earthly idea what it means? Google. Need to hire a carpet cleaner? Google. We use Google for so much. Your customers do too. And when they are looking for something like a kitchen remodel, they have lots and lots of questions. This means you need to create content on your website that answers those questions.

It also means you need to have the core information on your website that a prospect would want to know. Your website navigation (the menu bar at the top of your website) could look something like this:

- Home

- Services

- Process

- Portfolio

- About

- Blog

- Contact

All those pages represent opportunities and requirements for content. People are asking themselves three major questions when they are on your website:

1. Does your company do what they need (e.g., kitchen remodeling services)?

2. Do they trust you and feel like they want to do business with you?

3. Does it fit their budget?

The more content you have that supports these three questions, the better chance you have of them reaching out and wanting to start a discussion.

Your website content builds credibility for you.

SEARCH ENGINE OPTIMIZATION

Search engine optimization (SEO) is an extremely complex topic, and it's always changing. As of the writing of this book, it's reported that there are over two hundred ranking factors that Google looks at when trying to determine how to rank your website versus other websites.

The other fun part about SEO is that Google doesn't tell us what all the two hundred factors are. They tell us some things, but the rest is left to testing, measuring, and a little guesswork.

I like to say that SEO is part art, part science. It is the practice of increasing both the quantity and quality of traffic to your website through organic search results (nonpaid traffic). Aside from brand, SEO is one of the most critical pieces of the online marketing puzzle. If you aren't being found on search engines like Google and Bing, it's going to be tough to grow your business online. And as we move into the future, SEO will only become more critical. As consumers, we continue to become more and more reliant on Google rather than our own friends and family for recommendations, information, and just about anything.

We aren't going to be able to cover all two hundred ranking factors in this book, but I have included some additional resources on SEO at the end if you're interested in doing a deeper dive.

However, we are going to cover several elements that you can control when building and working on your website. Let's start with technical SEO.

Warning: This part of the book gets pretty technical. If you're not interested in getting super technical, I recommend skipping to the "Local SEO" section. Even if you don't want to read this section, I recommend skimming the headers to get familiar with some of the components.

On-Page Technical SEO

If your site's load time is too slow or the readability of your pages isn't up to par, search engines are going to ignore your page. Optimizing your technical and on-page SEO are ways to keep your site relevant.

Optimized Images

Harness the potential of your images. As a remodeler, your product and services speak best through pictures and video, and that means that your site should have a lot of them!

When uploaded properly, images and video content on your site will have a positive influence on your search engine ranking potential. But without intentional thought, these same images can cause numerous errors that search engine crawlers will ding your site for. You want to avoid this at all costs. The following steps explain how to avoid getting dinged.

Step 1: Resize your images

Photos from professional-grade cameras are typically upwards of 4000px wide, but if you upload hundreds of beautiful port-folio images to your site at this size, it will take forever for your website to load. Ideally, your pages should load in under three seconds; otherwise, your prospect will simply abandon the page and find something else that loads more quickly. In fact, 40 percent of users will abandon a page that does not load in under three seconds.

You can resize images in a variety of programs; it doesn't have to be anything fancy. The generic photo editing program on your PC or Mac (like Paint) will be able to accomplish this task with no problem. Figure 1 shows common sizes of images.

Figure 1.

Step 2: Optimize and compress your images

After resizing your images, it is time to rid them of the unnecessary metadata that is stored in the file. You can do this by
merely dragging and dropping the file(s) into an image com-
pression program. My two go-tos are www.TinyPNG.com and
www.ResizeImage.net.

The goal is to get your file size to be less than 100KB. This
is harder to do for images that are 1200px wide, but it is still
what you should be shooting for. Often you can run your
compressed image through the image compressor a second
time and shave off a little bit more from the file size without
losing image quality.

We have one more step before we can upload the image to
the website.

Step 3: Rename your images

Image titles like "IMG_0024" are extremely common on sites
that have a lot of images because it just doesn't seem worth it
or relevant to rename every single image. However, I promise
it is worth it because the SEO items that move the needle most
are the detailed ones. When a search engine crawler reads the
HTML of your site, they read the title and alt text associated
with your images (and videos) and use that information to further determine what the page is about.

Renaming your images to the associated service and your
location before uploading them to your site increases your site's
search engine ranking potential because including relevant keywords in your image's URL will make it more likely that search

engine crawlers will find and deliver your image to users in their search results. Here is an example of an appropriate file name: "modern-kitchen-design-denver-colorado".

Step 4: Upload to the site and include image alt text

Not taking the time to rename images and include image alt text is the #1 missed opportunity for targeting keywords and key phrases with the images on your website. When you upload an image to your website (after renaming it), be sure to set the alt text to be an even more descriptive explanation of the image than your already descriptive, SEO-optimized image title. This way, if the image does not load, the alt text will display on the page and tell users what type of image was supposed to display.

The alt text doesn't have to be much. Something that describes the picture and includes the location your company is targeting and the services your company offers will help improve your technical SEO. Figures 2, 3, and 4 are some examples.

**Figure 2: Mid-Century Modern Remodel in Buckhead
by Copper Sky Renovations.**

Figure 3: Tear Down Custom Build Project by GTG Builders.

**Figure 4: Four Level Graduate Hospital Rowhome
by Bellweather Design-Build.**

Writing alt text in these ways ensures you meet the following criteria:

- Provides content that screen readers use to help the blind and visually impaired interact with websites.

- Explains what is in the picture, so if the picture doesn't load for some reason, users are able to imagine what kind of picture is being shown.

- Targets the location of and services provided by your business in a smooth way.

- Provides search engine crawlers with content to use when populating image search results.

You'll want to write alt text on all of your images.

Figure 5 recaps how to optimize images.

DO

✔ DO resize your images to be no larger than 1200px wide
  - Full width on page: 1200px wide
  - Two-column layout: 600px wide
  - Small image for within text: 300–400px wide

✔ DO optimize your resized images to less than 100KB using TinyPNG.com

✔ DO rename your images to be descriptive and include a target key phrase and your company's location

✔ DO copy descriptive image title into the alt text field

DO NOT

✘ DO NOT upload images to your site straight from your professional photographer

✘ DO NOT upload images that are MBs large; aim for less than 100KB even though it is not always achievable

✘ DO NOT leave your image name as the default item number from your camera

✘ DO NOT leave the alt text field blank

Figure 5: Dos and don'ts of image optimization.

And if you've been debating whether or not to hire a professional photographer, the answer is yes.

Heading Structure

Dividing your content into sections and keeping a proper heading structure are great ways to make your content more readable for search crawlers and your web visitors alike.

What to Do

Some general rules of thumb when it comes to using H tags and P tags (headings and paragraph denotations in your website pages, blog posts, and landing pages) are

1. Always use only one heading 1 (H1) tag per page.

2. Keep headings in descending order.

3. Use a heading every 200–300 words.

4. Use headings as structural guides, not as ways to style your text.

1. Always use only one H1 tag per page

Your H1 tag is the title of your blog or main topic of your website page. This is the primary heading that search engines will use to determine what your page is about. If you have multiple H1 tags, your topics are competing on the page, and the search engine crawlers will not connect the content on your page together.

2. Keep headings in descending order

Headings should always descend in order and not skip a heading level. However, you can skip when they are ascending. Think about college term papers:

Good

H1—Home Remodeling

H2—Cost of Remodeling a Home

H2—Mistakes to Avoid

H3—Tips for Hiring the Right Contractor

H4—Do Your Research

H2—How Long It Takes to Remodel

Bad

H1—Home Remodeling

H3—Cost of Remodeling a New Home

H2—Mistakes to Avoid

H4—Tips for Hiring the Right Contractor

H2—Do Your Research

H4—How Long It Takes to Remodel

In the good example, there is a clear path that the information digs deeper into. When you have finished explaining the subtopics, you can move on to the next topic with a new H2.

In the bad example, search engine crawlers are not able to follow a clear path from the parent topic through subtopics and back out again. In their eyes, nothing looks connected.

Notice that in the example of a poor heading structure, the last two points are connected ("Do Your Research" and "How Long It Takes to Remodel"), but those are not the points that are truly related. Instead, the related points, as seen in the example of a good heading structure, are "Do Your Research" as a tip for hiring the right contractor, and then separate from both of those is "How Long It Takes to Remodel."

Moral of the story: Be nice to the search engine crawlers and keep your heading tags in descending order.

3. Use a heading every 200–300 words

Not only does using headings and subheadings every 200–300 words help organize your thoughts, it also helps readers follow your writing. In addition, it helps crawlers know exactly what your content is about, and it is becoming increasingly important with the rise of "jump to" link search results (aka fraggles).

4. Use headings as structural guides, not as a way to style your text

If you use a website builder, like WordPress, Wix, Squarespace, GoDaddy, or any variety of other platforms, you likely see a text editing box when you go to add content to a page, which looks something like Figure 6.

Figure 6: Text editing box example.

There is a text-styling option where you can set a heading or paragraph style. It is common to use this feature as a way to style text, but that is not what it is for. It may not seem like a big deal, but here's why this can mess up your SEO:

1. Search engines use H tags (heading denotations) to quickly determine what a website page is about as they decide which results to show to researchers.

2. There are two main files that make up your website as you see it visually, the HTML file and the CSS file:

    a. The HTML file houses the content on the page in a raw, unstyled form.

    b. The CSS file is the styling sheet for your page and styles the content in your HTML file based on IDs.

If you are using the heading settings (See Figure 6.) as a way to style your content instead of as a way to tell search engine crawlers what the page is about, you can end up with something that looks like Figure 7.

Figure 7: Text editing box with heading example.

It is common for people to want to make a cool quote bigger, so they use a bigger heading, even though it should just be paragraph text made larger.

And search crawlers don't associate your subpoint with the real parent point. In Figure 7, search crawlers would associate "subpoint" with "Cool quote I want you to see." This confuses the crawler because you really wanted the quote to be larger (not associated with a heading). Anytime you want something to be aesthetically larger, make sure you don't tag it as an H1, H2, etc. Just increase the font size. Your heading structure should follow your outline, just like a book or research paper.

Page Content

The content on your page is another important SEO and ranking factor. Google and other search engines like to see that your page has value and relevance to the keywords you're targeting. Search engines want their users to be satisfied when they produce a search term and click on a result in the search engine. This means your page needs to have added value that answers users' questions.

For Google to rank your page as a quality page, which will bump up your Google ranking status, you should write at least three hundred words on your page. Any page with fewer than three hundred words will be seen by Google as not useful for users, and therefore Google won't rank the page as high. For shorter pages, try to shoot for between five and seven hundred words. For longer, more encompassing pages, strive for a thousand to two thousand words. The more words on the page, the more useful Google deems your content, and your ranking potential increases.

Another essential aspect of page content is relevance and keywords. How relevant to a certain keyword is your page? Do you provide quality information on the subject or is your page about something completely different than your keywords in your headings, page title, and meta description? Google will notice and dock your rankings if your page isn't consistent with relevant content. You may be tempted to use a variety of keywords related to a topic, but Google sees this as keyword stuffing, and your page will be penalized. You should use keyword variations throughout your text, so Google knows that you're staying on the same or a similar subject.

User Experience

Everything related to the way your website or webpage ranks in Google boils down to its overall user-friendliness. There is a lot of debate about which ranking factors matter the most to move the needle for your SEO, but when you look behind the shouting and pointing of fingers, you see that at the end of the day, Google rewards websites that engage their users best by providing quality content and answers to searchers' questions.

So should you care about:

- Decreasing page load time?

- Decreasing bounce rate?

- Optimizing time on page and page views per session?

- Decreasing Search Console errors?

- Implementing internal linking strategies?

Yes, because everything in the list above is directly reflective of your user experience, make sure everything on your website is for the benefit of your user because that will help your SEO most. Here's an example of traffic growth as a result of implementing these types of SEO strategies.

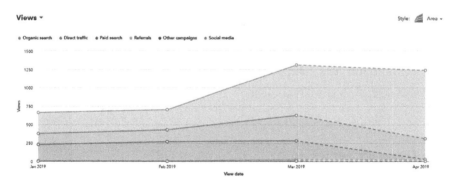

Figure 8: Traffic growth.

Notice the following line moving upwards. This represents traffic from Google search which means more of your prospects are finding you as they do research.

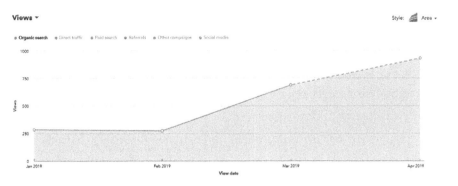

Figure 9: Organic traffic growth.

Keyword Targeted SEO Efforts

Keyword targeting is an important way to keep your web pages relevant, and it's mostly a matter of making sure the phrases your target audience is searching online are the phrases you use in your web content.

Keyword Research

Some people say keyword targeting is dead, but rather it has evolved. Remember how everything about your website should be focused on improving user experience? The same principle applies here.

The keywords and key phrases you target should be based on how you can provide value to a researcher who finds your page. Keyword stuffing—putting as many keywords on a page as you can—is a big no-no. Understanding the why behind your target audience's search queries and crafting quality content to answer their questions is what you should try to accomplish.

If you aren't genuinely answering questions about bathroom remodeling costs on a page, don't try to keyword stuff those terms just to rank for that term or phrase. But if you do have a page about bathroom remodeling costs, by all means, harness that potential, because your users care about that info, and it will help them.

Understand and Answer People's Questions

There are lots of ways to figure out what people are searching for. You can use Google's Keyword Planner, SEMrush, Ahrefs, and other keyword research tools. But there are also several creative ways to ensure you're answering the user intent of search queries. This includes answering the questions you find in:

- Google's "People also ask" dropdowns
- Quora
- Reddit
- Answer the Public
- Houzz

For example, when people search for the phrase "build versus buy" in Google, you'll see a "People also ask" section with drop-down SERP (search engine results pages) answers to questions Google has deemed related to the "build versus buy" search query, as shown in Figure 10.

Figure 10: "People also ask" dropdown SERP.

This means that if you are writing a blog post on building versus buying a home in Virginia, for example, including answers to these "People also ask" questions boosts your potential to rank well for that post.

Internal Linking Strategies

Links are important for Google to determine the value of your web pages and also function by helping your own pages boost each other's value.

What is internal linking?

Internal linking is the SEO technique whereby you include links from one piece of your content to another relevant piece of content and vice versa. This might seem like unnecessary effort, but it will boost your ranking potential for a couple of reasons:

1. When you link content together, Google search crawlers recognize that the content is related. When Google sees that your site has content on a variety of topics related to home building or home remodeling in your location, it will see your site as more of an expert on the topic and will be more likely to pull your content into search queries. To do this, be sure you:

    a. Link content to your service pages

    b. Link content to other related blogs

    c. Link content to landing pages to capture leads

2. Internal linking increases user experience, which is another prominent factor in Google's decision of whether or not to display your content in search results.

    a. You increase the potential for users to visit multiple pages on your site in a session, which Google views as a positive sign that people like reading your stuff.

    b. You give people direction as to where to find additional answers to their questions that spawn off of the original post.

3. Internal linking reduces the risk of having orphaned pages, which Google will ding you for. Orphaned pages are pages that are published as part of your site that don't link to any other page, meaning search engines can find them, but users can't. And if users can't find them, it is a poor user experience, which again, is what Google cares most about.

4. When you link, you can drive more traffic to pages that convert leads but may not rank well organically. Not all content will be a winner for generating organic search traffic, but that doesn't mean it is not a good piece of content or a good

page for conversions. Internal linking can help increase direct traffic to high-converting pages that struggle to be seen in search results but help guide users down the funnel.

Local SEO

If you're a localized home builder or remodeler, you'll want to make sure you're targeting the people in your area who can utilize your services. In this section, we explore some simple tactics you can use to better target the area you serve.

Location, Location, Location: NAP Citations

Location specificity is vital for local remodelers. If you're not targeting the entire nation, you don't want to use generalized keywords that will attract customers in the wrong locations. One way to ensure you're hitting the right target audience is to ensure your SEO NAPs (name, address, and phone number) are correct and consistent throughout the web. NAPs can become inconsistent when your business moves, changes phone numbers, changes names, or the name or address is typed differently in different places across the web.

NAPs are important to your ranking factors because they reflect your online authority. If your NAPs are inconsistent, your authority is diminished and your business appears lower on search results, even if your content is exactly what a user is searching for.

It's easy to have inconsistencies in your NAPs because Google takes into account every mention of your business online. From your website to your social accounts and third-party directories, Google crawls everything. Even NAP discrepancies as seemingly trivial as "South 21st Street" versus "S. 21st Street" will negatively affect your authority and ranking.

Incorrect NAPs can also be frustrating for potential customers and cost you business if the user can't get ahold of you because of outdated, incorrect information.

Should you be checking your NAPs? If your business is less than a year old, and you've never moved locations or changed names or changed any other aspect of your business, then you're probably doing OK. However, if your business is older, you've likely changed at least one aspect of your business, and it would be a good idea to check on your NAPs.

Here's how you can do a quick search to see if you need to clean up your listings.

1. Visit Moz Local: https://moz.com/local/search

2. Type in your business name and zip code and click "Check my listing."

3. View your score: The higher your score, the more consistent and correct your NAPs are across all listings on the internet. Your goal should be 85 percent accurate or higher.

4. Check areas for improvement. View the Incomplete, Inconsistent, and Duplicate tabs to see where your business is lacking in the area of NAPs. Make note of your areas for improvement and fix the inconsistencies on each site manually or by purchasing Moz's citation cleanup. (It's worth it.)

Local Keyword Targeting/Location Targeting

Another way to ensure you're attracting the right people is to use location-specific keyword targeting. All this means is adding specific locations to top keywords so users in and around those areas can find your content more easily.

Target local keywords and locations by taking a strategic approach to your webpages. Think about the kind of topics potential customers would search for and present that information in a way your audience would likely search on Google. For example, if your clients frequently ask you questions about the timeline of remodeling a house, try writing a blog post titled "How Long Will My Kitchen Remodel Take in [insert city name here]?" Using the question format for the title of the post will help users find your information, as that is how they will search for answers to their questions. For more local keyword targeting blog post opportunities, take a look at "257 Effective Home Builder Blog Topic Ideas" located in the appendix.

Google My Business

Google My Business is the latest and greatest social network that will positively impact your rankings in the Google search engine. Keeping your Google My Business listing up to date with correct NAPs, photos, offers, posts, and reviews can mean the difference in where you rank on Google, especially against your competitors.

You should be updating your Google My Business listing weekly via the Google Posts section to include new photos, company news, special offers, and recent blog posts. Be sure to leave personalized responses to reviews and update business info when applicable, such as holiday hours or closures. Read more about perfecting your Google My Business listing with our "Complete Guide to Google My Business for Home Builders and Remodelers" located in the appendix.

Questions to Ask Before You Hire Someone to Do Your SEO

Now you know the importance of SEO, but you still don't have a lot of the know-how, or maybe you just don't have enough time to worry about SEO. If you decide to hire somebody to do your SEO for your company, make sure you're asking all the right questions.

1. Can I see some case studies or examples of other clients you've helped?

This question will help you get to know the company's process and go-to strategies and let you see firsthand the results their clients have had. Remember, your company is unique, so you can expect your results to be unique to your company.

2. Which keywords bring in the best search volume?

The answer to this question, like many SEO questions, will vary depending on your business, location, competitors, and several other factors. However, the company you plan to hire should know through research which keywords bring in the best search volume. Frequently, we see a high search volume for anything price-related, but there will be several other keywords based on your specific services and location that will have high-ranking potential.

3. How difficult will it be to beat out my competitors?

Again, this depends on many factors, including your website's age, domain authority, the content on your website, how many competitors are in your area, the SEO practices they have in place, and other SEO factors. When you're vetting potential companies to do your SEO, they should talk about auditing your competitors' online presence to be able to give you a better idea of what it will take to beat them out.

4. How quickly will I rank #1?

In all transparency, ranking #1 on Google can never be guaranteed and is most easily considered on an individual basis. Your ability to climb the Google ladder depends on which keywords you're looking to rank for and the digital footprint of your competitors. Your timeline will also depend on where you are currently ranking. If you're on the second page of Google, it will be a much quicker ride to #1 than if you're on the third, fourth, or fifth page. Your prospective SEO company should be able to give you a better estimate.

5. What keywords will I rank for?

Most people want to rank for every keyword, but that's not practical. Make sure the company you hire has a firm grasp of what's possible and what may be too far-fetched. Be sure the keywords they suggest you try to rank for support the search intent of your target audience who would be searching for the services you offer. The company should be able to give you a good list of ranking potential keywords and how difficult it will be to rank for each one.

6. Which strategies will you use?

There should be strategies and tactics in place by a company in order to help your website SEO and search-ranking potential. At Builder Funnel, we use a variety of methods depending on your business goals to create the best results for you. Here are some examples of tactics we use in our SEO practices:

- Performing a website audit to evaluate:
    - Image optimization
    - Headings
    - Ranking keywords (current vs. potential)
    - Meta tags
    - Meta descriptions
    - Broken links
- Social media audit
- Content and user experience audit

SEO Recap and Next Steps

SEO is critical for remodelers who are looking to gain a competitive advantage on search engines such as Google. Remember the three main factors to implement in your SEO plan: technical SEO, keyword targeted SEO, and local SEO.

LEAD CONVERSION

Nothing happens until something gets sold. Let's talk about lead conversion. This is one of my favorite parts of the marketing funnel, but it's also one of the most underutilized in our industry. If you start implementing the techniques in this section, you'll leap ahead of your competition.

Before we jump in, I want you to think about the buying journey your prospect goes on before moving forward with a remodeling project. Let's say the end project is a $75,000 kitchen remodel.

The first step in your prospect's journey is not to find and contact a remodeler. Your prospect—let's call her Mary—starts her journey in her own mind. She's dreaming about having friends over for parties. She's imagining making meals for her family and people sitting at the island on those bar stools that swivel. There's a double oven, which makes Thanksgiving a cinch. She searches design trends on Instagram. She looks at potential themes for her kitchen on Pinterest. She reads blogs and gathers ideas and information.

What if Mary lands on your website? She's certainly not ready to talk to you yet. Her dream isn't at the stage where it can become a reality. If your website operates like most remodeling websites, she's going to look at some of your portfolio pages, read some blog posts (if you have any), and then she'll leave.

Missed opportunity. This was your opportunity to engage with Mary. This was your opportunity to start a conversation and be a part of her buying journey. But you missed it.

To avoid missing the opportunity, you need top of the funnel lead conversion. Let's rewind a minute. Mary is still on your portfolio page. She's looking at amazing photos and really likes your work and your style. Then something catches her eye. It's a button for downloading a kitchen design guide. She's interested. She clicks the button and is taken to a page with a form. She enters her name and email and downloads the guide. Lead captured!

Now don't start pestering Mary and asking her to set up a call. She's not ready for that. However, she is ready for more information.

By giving something of value to Mary, you do two things: You capture her information, and you get your brand in front of her and become a part of her journey. She's now aware of you.

You now have the opportunity to continue to add value to her journey by educating her on the remodeling process and updating her on the current design trends and new home technology available.

Mary's journey might take a few months or a few years. We don't know that yet, but we know you're a part of it now. You can set yourself apart from the competition and start to earn her trust and, eventually, her business.

Everyone is sleeping on the top of the funnel, but that's where the money is made. Fast forward six to twelve months, and you have everyone who is currently ready to buy *plus* all the dreamers from six to twelve months ago who are ready to move forward.

Widen the top of the funnel, and you'll widen the bottom of the funnel.

ToFu, MoFu, BoFu

When we break down the marketing funnel, we have three major stages:

1. Top of the Funnel (ToFu)

2. Middle of the Funnel (MoFu)

3. Bottom of the Funnel (BoFu)

How do we know where someone is on the journey? Today, it can be challenging to figure that out, and buyers will often jump all over the funnel. Their journey isn't a straight line. That being said, there are a few identifiers that can help us figure out where these people are and how we should be helping them.

Top of the Funnel

As we just discussed, buyers at this stage are dreaming. Over the years, I've found there are three main unknowns at this stage:

1. Will she buy?

2. When will she buy?

3. Who will she buy from?

It's tempting to discount leads at this stage of the funnel because you don't know if they will ever buy. That's one of the biggest unknowns. However, there is a percentage of top-of-the-funnel leads that always buy. Serious buyers all start at the dreaming phase and then move on from there.

Middle of the Funnel

Once Mary has transitioned from dreaming, she enters the middle of the funnel. At this stage, she is trying to figure out logistically how to make her dream happen. She's interested in learning about cost, process, timeline, and how to find the right company to work with on her remodel.

There are two unknowns left at this stage:

1. When will she buy?

2. Who will she buy from?

It's important at this stage to be delivering content that helps Mary understand how her dream will come true. Cost is an important topic to cover here. Talking about cost and pricing on your website does a few critical things for you. It starts to earn you trust. You're showing a level of transparency that Mary appreciates.

It also helps you qualify your leads. If you specialize in kitchen remodels between $75,000 and $150,000, and you're talking about that range on your website, it helps you weed out leads who were looking for a $30,000 kitchen. They'll read about your cost and pricing and leave. This is exactly what you want. You don't want to waste time talking to these leads when you know they won't ever buy from you due to cost.

Finally, cost content actually draws lots of traffic to your website. When Mary googles something like "how much does a kitchen remodel in Denver cost?" your content pulls her in. Just make sure you're giving a full answer to the question on your website and providing really useful information.

Talk about why it might be on the low end (lesser finishes, less moving of walls, less square footage, etc.). Talk about why it might be on the high end of the range as well. Show examples of kitchens on the low end, in the middle, and on the high end. Think about what you would want to know and see if you were researching the same thing.

If you put yourself in your prospect's shoes, you'll create incredible content that not only attracts tons of leads but also weeds out the leads you don't want to spend time with.

Bottom of the Funnel

The bottom of the funnel is where all but one unknown has been removed, and that unknown is: Who will she buy from?

At this stage, you're working to differentiate yourself from the competition and the lead has probably entered your sales process to some degree. She may have had an initial phone call with you or your company or even one or two in-person meetings.

If you've been a part of Mary's journey from the top of the funnel down, you're already in a good position to win the job, but there are a few more things you can do at this stage to help seal the deal.

Having video testimonials along with written testimonials on your website will really help you stand out. Video testimonials can be tough to get, but if you can have three to five of these on your website and social media, it will help your prospects get to know you and get a feel for what it's like to work with you through a trusted third party—your past customer.

Make sure you display other trust-builders on your website, like any awards you've won or mentions in the media. These can really stand out to your prospects and help them feel like they are making a safe choice.

At the end of the day, your prospects are trying to avoid a bad decision and a bad experience, rather than trying to have a great experience. The safer you can make them feel, the better your opportunity to earn their business.

And, finally, this stage is commonly where marketing and sales blur together. Sales training and sales skills are topics for other books, but your sales process and your ability to close business will heavily impact this stage. That being said, doing a great job at the top, middle, and bottom on the marketing side will set you up for great success in the sales process even if your company hasn't mastered sales yet.

Bonus: Lead-Nurturing Campaigns

As you start to generate more and more leads through your website, it can become a burden to follow up with all of them manually. It's especially tough when you know many of these leads won't be buying for six to twelve months.

Let's talk about how you can make these leads feel like you're personally following up with them but in a way that is automatic for you: automated lead-nurturing campaigns.

I think the best way to explain this is through an example. In 2011, I hosted a webinar about blogging strategies. Dozens of remodelers and custom builders attended the webinar to learn about how we were using blogging to draw in ideal customers. After the webinar, I offered the attendees a chance to chat with me one on one to discuss how we could help them implement the strategies talked about in the webinar.

One of my conversations was with Andrew, a custom home builder and remodeler. We looked at his website and found there were big opportunities for improvement. The website was outdated, and there was no search engine optimization strategy or content creation strategy, and he wasn't capturing leads in research mode.

After our initial review of his website, we decided it would make sense to build a marketing plan to address these issues and move the company forward. Andrew wanted to grow, and he understood that growth could come from the internet.

I built a plan based on what was working for other builders and remodelers like him, and we circled back around to talk through the plan together. Everything was making sense, and it seemed like we were going to do business. I sent Andrew the plan after our call, and something weird happened. He disappeared. I know you've probably never had this happen in the sales process. A meeting goes well. All signs are pointing to moving forward, but then the prospect disappears.

I followed up diligently for a few months like any good salesperson should do, but I also put Andrew on our regular email program. This ensured he was always seeing our content. He got notified when we published new blog posts on our website. He was alerted when we hosted more webinars. He was seeing our content and my face on a monthly basis at a minimum. Although Andrew didn't reply to the personal emails I sent to check in with him, I continued to see him open our regular marketing emails and engage with our content.

Over the next two years, Andrew opened and clicked many of our emails, and he re-visited the website several times. Then he finally responded. He said he wanted to talk again about his website and digital marketing efforts. We got back on the phone and went through the process again. We discussed his goals, looked at his website to see if anything had changed, and updated the old plan we had originally put together.

All things were pointing to working together, but then the same thing happened! He disappeared on me again. I started the same process of following up personally, and he continued to receive our content. Fast forward another two years, and we're back on the phone. This time, Andrew decided to move forward with us, and now we've been working together for over two years.

There are a couple of points I want to highlight in this story. The first is that persistence pays off, but you don't have to manually be persistent. Almost all of my follow-up was automated. He was receiving our email newsletter and other emails that were going out to our entire list of prospects and customers. These emails added value. They aren't salesy or pushy. They deliver content that helps the recipient. They deliver content that earns trust with the prospect because we're regularly giving out information that will help improve their website's traffic and lead generation and help them grow their business. We do this because we know if someone wants to do what we're telling them on their own, they aren't a good fit for us anyway. Those who don't want to do what we are telling them on their own get a ton of value from us. We're earning their trust.

When Andrew and I talked that third time, about six years after our first conversation, he wasn't even considering another option. We had provided so much value to him and earned his trust, but we did it at scale. It didn't require hours and hours of personal time. Yes, I spent time with Andrew in the sales process, but it was the marketing machine in the background that was staying in front of him regularly.

This process works the same for you. Your prospects may be dreaming about their home remodeling project for years. Don't dismiss a prospect as junk just because the timing isn't right. Use the opportunity to build trust and build your future pipeline. That way, you've always got a full funnel of prospects—some who are ready to buy today, some who are ready to buy tomorrow, and some who are ready months or years from now. Keep the top of your funnel full, and you'll keep the bottom full too.

Targeted Email-Nurturing Campaigns

What I just described is a generic way of nurturing and staying in front of prospects and leads. It's extremely effective, but we can also do better. What I'm going to walk you through next is a more specific, more targeted way of nurturing leads that will take your conversion to the next level.

Let's say Mary visits your website and is researching kitchen design trends. She finds a few of your blog posts on kitchen remodeling, and she's browsing your kitchen portfolio. She spots a call to action for a free kitchen design guide. She clicks the button and is taken to a landing page where she fills out a form and converts. From here, we have two options. We can send her our regular email newsletters and email blasts and nurture her that way, or we can use a more targeted approach.

Because we know she is researching kitchens, we can now drop her into an automated, predesigned sequence of emails about kitchens. The first email should go out automatically as a thank you to Mary for downloading the free guide and provide an easy access link to the PDF.

Your second email can go out a couple of days later. In this email, you can again thank her for downloading the free guide and offer up a few links to some kitchen design–related blog posts she may not have discovered.

A few days later, another email goes out to Mary. This time, the email has links to blog posts focused on FAQs like process and timeline, such as "How Long Does It Take to Remodel a Kitchen?" or "What Does the Kitchen Remodeling Process Look Like?"

Several days later, Mary gets another email containing links to some blog content around budget and pricing.

This sort of targeted email campaign can go on and on. I typically recommend a series of three to seven emails that go out every two or three days. The idea is that you want Mary to get super familiar with you, as close to her point of conversion as possible.

You should also include a postscript in your email to offer her a meeting. This typically looks something like this: "P.S. If you ever want to chat about your project, just reply to this email or give me a call at 999-999-9999."

As people continue to receive value from you, your credibility goes up, and their comfort level with you goes up. When their comfort level increases, they are more likely to reach out and book a meeting to talk about their project.

This targeted sequence allows you to deliver exponential value to your prospect because they already told you the topic they were interested in by downloading your free guide on kitchens.

Your prospects will continue to receive your email newsletter and generic nurturing content. These emails are extremely targeted, and they should look like one-to-one emails coming from you or whoever is in the sales role. This gives the appearance that you're writing the email just for them, which you are—you just pre-wrote them.

I've found that these targeted nurturing sequences can lead to a higher conversion of appointments set than a generic nurturing approach, but it does take more time and effort to create them upfront, and you need the correct technology. Once you start putting in place automation like this, you'll never want to go back!

Build a Presence on Social Media

Social media is an ever-evolving landscape. Platforms come and go, algorithms shift daily, and the user bases continue to skyrocket. Every day on social media is a chance to meet a new lead, learn about your audience's buyer journey, engage with a client, or even research your target audience. With so many ways to use social media, how do you know what's right for you? When used properly, social media can be one of your best sales tools.

Let's break it down.

Why Should You Use Social Media to Grow Your Remodeling Business?

There's a reason more and more companies are using social media to market their products and services: It works! Social media is everywhere. Even if your business isn't attracting the quality or quantity of leads you expected from social media, there are still plenty of reasons to keep up on social networking platforms. Social media isn't going away anytime soon, and you need to tap into this (mostly) free opportunity as much as possible to grow your business. Social media is the digital way to do what your company has always done—get the word out.

The key lies in constructing an effective social media marketing strategy. There is no way to appeal to your followers without posting content. You should be updating your accounts with engaging content that will build a relationship with your followers. Responding individually to supporters across networks will give your followers a sense that you care about them, and that will make them more likely to stick around and continue engaging.

Use Social Media to Humanize Your Brand and Engage with People

The point of social media is to showcase what you can do, how you do it, and whether you do it well enough for people to buy from you. It is a natural form of communication between your business and consumers. Relatable content is key to engaging with consumers on social media, so ensure your consumers can identify with your posts. This type of content can also help humanize your brand and shows consumers your people, your passion, and your pride.

Remember, people go to social media for three things:

- To connect with people (and if you're lucky, your business).

- To learn about something. What can you teach your followers about your industry?

- To be entertained. Time-lapse videos, home walk-through videos, and gorgeous photos are great entertaining content.

Use Social Media to Generate Trust and Brand Awareness

Consumers need to know your brand exists before they can purchase your services, and one way to inform them is to share on social platforms. Social media marketing also helps to establish your legitimacy as a home remodeling contractor and can help consumers begin to trust your company as a qualified builder. Here are some things you can do to better serve potential clients:

- Build legitimacy by posting a real photo of the business owner, the contractor, or the director on your profile

- Provide your real name and contact info

- Develop your personal brand with regular posts and by responding directly to comments and questions

- Occasionally publish posts that are more personal and have nothing to do with business

Use Social Media to Gain More Website Traffic and Leads

Facebook and other social media networks allow you to distribute highly targeted social media advertisements to the target audience that is right for your remodeling business, which can be more affordable per lead than other means of advertising. Your content will also help generate leads as you continue to share helpful information.

You can also promote your own content through social media with the hope of going viral and increasing that page's SEO value. You can announce new blog posts, a free eBook download, or advice and information about building or remodeling in your area. Make sure these posts are teasers, with the end goal of getting users to click through to your site to read the full content.

How to Use Facebook for Remodelers

Facebook is the most widely known and most consistently used social media platform in existence. Roughly two billion people use Facebook, and over eighty million of those users are on the mobile app. In fact, studies have shown that 83 percent of women and 75 percent of men use Facebook, and the age range of 18–29 is the most engaged group on the platform. When you consider that women are likely your audience's decision-maker and that the age group you have already been spending money to reach is waiting to be tapped, it seems very foolish not to be where they are!

Where to Start: Facebook Basics

How to Create (and Optimize)
a Company Facebook Page

In order to start a company Facebook page, you must already be a user. The company page is tacked on to your profile so that when you login, you can access both profiles at the same time. Once you are logged in, select the dropdown arrow in your menu and scroll down to Create Page. Facebook will begin a guided process of asking you for information to fill out your company page.

Here are some tips for optimizing your Facebook business page:

- Start your page as a local business. This will help Facebook optimize your posts toward a local audience.

- Use your logo as the profile image.

- Use an image from your most stunning project for your cover photo.

- Be sure your correct contact information is included in your profile.

- Use a simple call to action on your profile such as "Learn More" or "Call Now."

- Include a link to your company website in your profile.

What Should Be Shared on Facebook?

Think of Facebook as a water cooler. Everyone is congregating, sharing stories and pictures, listening to one another, and fully engaged. It's a break from the real world, the workday grind, and a way to feel important while in line at Starbucks.

As a remodeler, Facebook is the perfect platform to share stories about your brand, your team, your clients, and your projects. There are dozens of posts that will be extremely popular on your company Facebook page:

- Project albums: Build albums of your projects, whether they're completed or still underway. Your target audience is using your Facebook page as a way to do research. They're learning if they like your brand, trust your team, and want their home to look like your "after" imagery. Your "before" and "during" imagery will also tell a story of their own, a story that the homeowners are living right now. Their current environment is your "before" photography.

- Team bios: Feature team members with a headshot and their bio. Better yet, give your team members a chance to feel a part of your brand and to buy in to your social media marketing by allowing them to build their own post about themselves and to respond to any comments that come in.

- Work events: Share your culture. Whether we like to admit it or not, your remodeling or contracting company can be difficult to differentiate from the competition. Sharing your culture on Facebook for your audience to see is a great way to differentiate yourself. From a coffee break team meeting to a Christmas festival, showcasing who you are and what you represent is a great way to engage your audience.

- Seminars: Do you host seminars at your office or showroom or online via webinars? Create an event on Facebook! This is the perfect way to easily reach a large audience and encourage them to come to an event.

- Your blog content: If you're blogging already for your remodeling business, you should be sharing every new blog post on Facebook. Keep in mind that Facebook's most recent algorithm updates are to protect their users from content saturation, so be sure that any blog post you share is something your users want to read and that your post is also high quality and engaging.

How Often Should You Post on Facebook?

Facebook is constantly editing and developing its algorithm to improve the user experience. So no matter what updates occur, as long as you are always posting with your audience and their user experience in mind, then you are working with the flow of traffic. Essentially, if you are posting when you know your audience is online, then your material will be seen.

As a general rule of thumb, Facebook is most popular in the mornings (before work), in the early afternoon (on a lunch break), and in the evenings (after work and into the night). If this is when your users are checking their newsfeeds, it is a good time to post and show up. Insert yourself into their buyer journey and post when they're online! With our years of experience in social media marketing for remodelers and builders, Builder Funnel recommends posting once a day on Facebook. But if that's too much, three to five times per week is a good start.

Consider your buyer personas. When are they online? When are they interacting with Facebook? If you have a client whom you have a strong relationship with, you can ask them for some insights such as when they're online, what kind of content they like seeing on Facebook, and any other questions that will help you post the right stuff at the right time.

You'll also want to keep in mind what you are posting and when. For example, is an interested homeowner going to make a decision on their lunch break? Don't go in for the ask at 11:54 a.m. on a Tuesday. Instead, share a helpful post about how to design the perfect entertaining space when building a new home. Go in for the ask on a Sunday afternoon when a prospect is doing their research and browsing in their area; share your Schedule a Consultation page from your website.

How to Interact with Facebook Users

Social media is so powerful because it allows companies to interact with leads and clients immediately. Gone are the days of leads scrubbing your website until they find the exact detail they are searching for. Now users expect to be able to find everything instantly—and that includes asking directly.

Facebook is the perfect platform for this engagement. It encourages people to contact a company directly by commenting on a post but also by sending a message. In fact, one of Facebook's dozens of ranking factors for your page is your response time on Facebook Messenger. The point of being on a social media platform to begin with is so that you can be social. Be sure to respond to messages you receive, and if possible, in a very timely manner.

Another ranking factor for Facebook is how engaged users are with your posts. The more comments and shares your post gets, the more Facebook recognizes it as good content. This is the kind of good content that it wants to share more prolifically, so your post's reach will increase with each comment. Friends of the commenter will be able to see the post in their newsfeed, which will then open their eyes to your company as well. A very powerful way to interact with your audience is to find new ways for them to comment on your post. If you're successful, remember to reply to their comments. This will increase that post's reach so that even more people see it.

Plus, high-engagement posts are perfect opportunities to grow your page's following and increase the reach your organic posts have.

Advertising and Lead Generation on Facebook

Now that you've mastered the basics of marketing on Facebook as a remodeler, you're ready to graduate to lead generation. This is the part of social media marketing that spreads past brand awareness and dives into conversion. After all, when you're putting so much effort into a single social media platform, you want to see the results.

Calls to Action on Facebook

You may have noticed that your company Facebook page has a call-to-action button on the right side of its banner image. While there are several call-to-action options, it's important to consider how your users are finding you. For example, if they're finding you while still doing research on remodeling, they may not be ready to call you. In that case, it's best to encourage them to learn more and send them to your blog or project portfolio. If most of your users are finding you on the Facebook mobile app, then including a Call Now button will make their research easier rather than having to search your social sites and website to find a piece of information. Mobile users are more likely to call than browser users.

If you're not sure which button to use, start simple and work your way up. Switch them up every few months to see which gets you the most leads. You're only one click away from editing your call to action.

Setting Up Services Pages

Buried in the left menu of your company Facebook page, you can build out your Services tab. Click into Services, click the button Add a Service, and start building out all of the services you offer. Of course, we recommend being up front about pricing. Let your leads self-qualify themselves; you don't want to waste your time on tire kickers.

Here are some examples of remodeler or contractor services you may want to add:

- Design consultation
- Kitchen remodeling
- Bathroom remodeling
- Whole-home remodeling
- Exterior remodeling
- Basement remodeling
- Additions

Creating and Moderating Groups on Facebook

Creating a private Facebook group is an incredibly powerful tool for your future marketing endeavors. If you have a group of clients or leads who are extremely engaged with your brand, you can leverage their excitement and honesty to influence others. You can also get priceless feedback about your content, branding, messaging, pricing, and more.

As a remodeler, creating Facebook groups for all of your homeowners who live in particular communities or neighborhoods is an incredible way to erase any buyer's remorse. All homeowners will have an instant network to meet neighbors, learn about local events, and even discover tax breaks in their particular area.

To create a group, locate the "..." next to Liked, Following, and Share below your cover photo and select Create Group from the dropdown menu. At Builder Funnel, we're huge fans of reaching out to people personally rather than with mass marketing, so we highly recommend you attach a personal note to each and every person you carefully choose to be in your group. After all, they are representing your brand!

Boosting Posts on Facebook to Increase Reach

One huge benefit to posting on Facebook as a company page is that you are able to turn existing posts into boosts or ads with a click of a button. One of the best ways to increase your reach, gain more clicks to links you share, or maximize a campaign is through boosting posts on Facebook.

You can quickly and easily add a target audience and a budget you're willing to spend to target that audience for a certain amount of time, and voilà! Your post has been boosted.

Developing and Implementing
a Facebook Ads Strategy

Beyond boosting posts, I also highly recommend developing a Facebook advertising strategy and implementing it immediately. Facebook Ads is still in its infancy, so these ads will cost much less per click than those with Google Ads. Paying for an audience or a click is currently far less expensive on Facebook than on Google, and now is the perfect time to start maximizing your advertising budget!

Facebook advertising is complex. You have several options for how to optimize your ads (for video views, for website clicks, for views on the post, etc.) and endless options when you are building out your audience. Here are a few of our recommendations to get you off the ground:

- Retargeting: A quick way to send out your first Facebook ad is to target your existing leads and clients. You can upload Excel spreadsheets as lists to build your audience. This is beneficial if you are trying to advertise for your current clients or leads to like your Facebook page, for example. It can also be the perfect audience if you are trying to re-engage your leads with a free eBook or a seminar event.

- Lead ads: This format of ads is ridiculously engaging and addictive. It is the perfect way to discover new leads and gain their email addresses directly from Facebook rather than asking them to leave the platform and fill out a form on your website.

- Pay-per-click: Both Google and Facebook give businesses the option to purchase PPC ads, but they operate differently. Google Ads work by showing your ad when specific keywords are searched. The targeting is based on immediate user search intent. Facebook Ads, on the other hand, target users by location, demographic, and interests to gain you clicks even when the user is not directly searching on a search engine. The targeting is based on passive information gathered about users and what solutions they could be looking for.

- Increasing reach: Another way you can utilize Facebook's advertising platform is to pay to show up in more newsfeeds. Essentially, you are able to handpick your audience (for remodelers, you could target those who like pages such as HGTV and who meet a certain income level) and then showcase specific promotions or content directly to that audience.

- Video views: As a remodeler or builder, one of your best methods for promoting yourself is through photography and open houses or events. What if you were able to create a slideshow of images of your newly remodeled home—essentially build a virtual open house tour—and then share it specifically to local homeowners in a specific neighborhood? That's the power of Facebook.

Analytics and Problem Solving on Facebook

Check Your Analytics

The first thing to check when it seems like Facebook just isn't the right platform is your analytics. After all, everything you do on Facebook is measurable. Check your Insights tab at the top of your company page to learn more about what's working and what isn't. Scroll along the entire left navigation to discover more information about your promotions, followers, likes, reach, page views, posts, events, videos, and more.

The only way to fix something that isn't working is to know what's broken. Digging into analytics will show you what's broken.

Check Your Reviews

Another reason you could have low engagement or reach on your Facebook page is if you have been dinged with negative reviews. It's just a fact of life; there will always be haters. And on social media, it's easy to leave a negative review even if it isn't true!

The best thing you can do when you get a negative review is to respond in a timely manner. And if you truly believe that the review is a bot or spam, then reach out to Facebook for Small Businesses immediately to dispute it.

How to Use Instagram Marketing for Remodelers

Instagram is one of the quickest rising social media platforms ever. Most other platforms had a gradual increase to popularity, but Instagram seemed to take over almost overnight. The simple platform makes it easy to captivate users and even easier to engage. As remodelers, this is the perfect platform to showcase your beautiful photography!

Roughly 71 percent of businesses are on Instagram, and 80 percent of Instagram users are currently following at least one business profile. In other words, if your remodeling business isn't already on Instagram, then your ideal leads are following your competitors instead. There are a variety of ways you can leverage Instagram to generate remodeling or building leads. According to Sprout Social, "as of March 2017, over 120 million Instagram users visited a website, got directions, called a business, emailed or direct-messaged a business."[1]

Instagram Marketing Basics

Instagram is probably the most streamlined social media profile you'll ever create. It's as simple as downloading the app, logging in, and going. Of course, we have plenty of tips on how to get started by optimizing your profile and posts.

---

1   "How Brands Use Instagram." https://sproutsocial.com/insights/instagram-stats/

How to Create (and Optimize)
Your Instagram Profile

After downloading the Instagram app and creating your profile, you can select the Settings wheel in the top right menu in order to build your profile into a business account. Follow the steps Instagram has already laid out to continue to convert your profile into a business page.

You will also be guided to attach other social media accounts to your Instagram account. If you are still developing your full social media strategy, you can come back to attaching other accounts later. If we're being honest, at Builder Funnel, we don't recommend sharing the same content on Facebook and Instagram. There is a reason they are two separate platforms—they have different audiences, and each audience wants to see something different.

Continue optimizing your profile by adding your logo as your profile image. This will eradicate any confusion a user has when trying to search for you.

Next, fill out your profile information. This will include a limited number of characters (roughly 240 characters) to describe yourself. When writing about yourself on Instagram, keep in mind that this isn't the time to let your sales hat shout over your marketing mind. Take this opportunity to empathize and connect with users. Once they call you, you can put your sales hat back on.

What Should Be Shared on Instagram

Instagram users are there for the photography. There's little else to see, right? Wrong.

Instagram is about stories. You should be using Instagram to share content that tells a story:

- Beautiful, professional photography: If you don't have a lot of imagery yet, we recommend you share each picture one at a time over a couple of weeks rather than posting multiple images at once. This will increase your fan base consistently over time and will continue to increase your engagement on each image.

- Multiple images: On Instagram, you have the option to post a single image or multiple images at a time as a single post. Consider posting multiple images as being similar to creating a Facebook album. They work well to showcase before and after imagery in the same post. They also work well to showcase an entire project in one post rather than uploading each image as a separate post.

- Behind the scenes: Instagram is the perfect place to tell a behind-the-scenes story, such as team meetings or client projects that are still under construction. Remember that users are trying to learn more about you. They're trying to decide if you're the right company to work with and if they see themselves in your clientele.

- Stories: These are quick shots that erase after twenty-four hours, just like Snapchat only built into the

Instagram app. If you're feeling daring, edit the
images and add hashtags or tag people. If not, just
take a quick shot of your cuppa joe in the morning
and say hi! Instagram users just want to see what
you're really like.

- Filters: They can make anything look beautiful, but
  they can also make anything beautiful look cheesy. If
  you already have professional photography, you can
  lay off the filter editing (#nofilter). If you used your
  iPhone to snap a few quick pics at your last job site,
  spice up your pictures a bit when posting with a filter.

- Videos: Instagram users are obsessed with video. This
  is the perfect place to upload a video (as long as it's
  square and under sixty seconds) to share with your followers. Some Instagram video ideas for your business
  are a professional photography slideshow of a newly
  remodeled home and a quick interview with your chief
  designer discussing design challenges and goals for a
  new project you took on.

- Hashtags: As Builder Funnel teammate Danielle Russell
  would say, "I'm seriously so glad you asked because I'm
  sick of seeing your hashtags." Using hashtags properly
  on Instagram will help your content be found by those
  who are directly searching for it, such as #homeremod-
  eler and #dallasremodeling.

How Often Should You Post on Instagram

Growing your followers on Instagram requires consistent posting. This means that it's critical to keep posting over time in order to show up in people's searches. If you have a ton of imagery, you can post pretty regularly. You may even want to add a few projects (as multiple images or as single images at a time) right away so that users know what kind of pictures they'll be seeing moving forward if they follow you.

If you don't have a lot of imagery, post once or twice a week. It's fine to start small! If each image and caption tells a story, then it doesn't matter if you're not posting daily—you're posting what Instagram users look forward to discovering. Remember, quality over quantity.

Because of the nature of the Instagram algorithm, time of day doesn't matter much for posting. Similar to Facebook, however, we recommend posting when people are online— before work, during lunch, and in the evenings after work. Instagram is extremely popular late into the night for those who have already climbed into bed but just aren't quite ready to sleep yet.

How to Interact on Instagram

Just like Facebook, Instagram is an extremely social platform. There are a few important ways to remember to interact with your followers on Instagram that will make sure they feel appreciated and engaged. And before you ask how responding to an Instagram direct message could help someone choose to buy a remodeling service from you, I'd like to remind you that millennials—your ideal buyers—grew up in a world where research is largely conducted on social media platforms.

Here are the key ways to interact on Instagram:

- Direct messages: Instagram users can send your business profile a message. Sometimes these messages are compliments of your work (in which case you should respond), and sometimes these messages are bots asking you to read their soon-to-be *NYT* bestseller.

- Comments: If your followers comment on your posts, you should always respond. When others see that you respond to comments, they'll feel more welcome to comment on your posts as well. It's a snowball effect of goodness that increases your post's popularity and will help it reach the top of search results on Instagram.

- Instagram stories: Clients may tag you in their pictures during and after a renovation. If they tag you in a story, you will receive a notification. This is the perfect time to turn a client into a raving fan by responding with how much you enjoyed working with them and that you hope they'll recommend you to friends and family as they begin their own home remodeler search. Further, leverage your own Instagram stories by snapping a quick pic with your clients during the stages of the project. Mention your clients by using the @

symbol and typing their name, so you can also leverage their network in direct connection to your account. (If you want to go above and beyond with your marketing, you can present a collage of these photos as a house-warming gift at the end.)

Advertising and Lead Generation on Instagram

Because Facebook owns Instagram, you will have the option to optimize and share the same ads on Facebook as on Instagram without any extra work. This is a great way to increase your followers on Instagram.

Lead Generation on Instagram

Instagram prides itself on its simplicity. In an effort to maintain this, there aren't many ways to optimize your business page for lead generation. However, there a couple of ways to make sure you engage those who are truly interested in your brand:

- Link in bio: The only clickable link you can have on Instagram is a single link in your bio. That means that when you post, you can't link to a blog or website page. If you're desperate, you can write out your URL, but because Instagram is an app, the likelihood of someone copying and pasting your link into a separate browser and leaving the Instagram app entirely is very low. You can continually update the link in your Instagram bio to see what engages your fans—typically your website home page is a great starting place. You can also use a tool like Linktree, which allows you to put multiple links in your bio.

- Promote: Just like boosting a Facebook post, you have the opportunity to boost any of your posts that are performing well. We recommend waiting to see which post performs well organically and then putting a budget behind it to increase its reach.

Analytics on Instagram

Check Your Analytics

When logged in as your business profile, you can check your Instagram analytics. This is helpful to see which posts are performing best, what days you tend to gain more followers, how many clicks your chosen URL receives, and what your audience demographics currently look like.

If any of these analytics don't represent what you are hoping to achieve, then test! Try new filters on your images, try posting at a different time of day, do more in-depth hashtag research. There are plenty of methods to try to increase your Instagram engagement.

Houzz Marketing for Remodelers

Houzz has been a popular social media marketing platform since 2009. While its popularity among remodelers and contractors has been on the decline, it is still very popular for the end-user—those searching for a contractor or remodeler. According to 2019 data, Houzz boasts 40 million users and over 1.5 million local professionals (such as yourselves).[2]

As Houzz's business model has shifted to lean heavily on benefiting their Pro Plus accounts and to offer a variety to its end users, its popularity among contractors and remodelers is dwindling under cries of commoditizing the industry. For now, users enjoy being able to search for local professionals, sifting through project imagery, and researching costs and trends on the site.

Houzz is also relevant for custom builders. While you will have fewer projects to share by nature of the business, it is still an excellent way to share images of your completed homes—especially once they're staged.

Houzz Basics

Your Houzz profile will have three primary functions: showcasing project imagery, responding to messages and questions, and developing a system to get reviews on your profile.

---

2   "'Before we knew it this little website had 350,000 users.'" https://www.bbc.com/news/business-48395181

How to Create and Optimize Your Houzz Profile

Similarly to both Facebook and Instagram, we recommend building your professional profile using your logo as your profile picture. Your cover photo should either be a picture of your team together or a particularly impressive project. Keep in mind that this is likely someone's first impression of you if they've landed on your profile page.

In an effort to keep your profile looking active and engaging, we recommend updating your cover photo seasonally. Several studies have shown that people try to see themselves in a set of clientele before making a decision. Updating your cover photo seasonally will also aid in showcasing the type of project users are currently searching for as well. For example, you might post decks in the summer, three-season rooms in the spring, and kitchen renovations before the winter holidays.

As you continue to fill out basic information on your profile, Houzz will highlight what information to continue providing to optimize your profile. Houzz recommends building out several projects, collaborating with clients on ideabooks, requesting reviews from clients, and responding to questions and messages.

What Should You Share on Houzz?

Houzz offers a few ways to share your content with your audience. The most common mistakes we see in sharing on Houzz are easily avoidable. Here's where you should focus your content.

- Houzz projects: This section of your Houzz profile requires professional photography of completed projects. This is not the time to showcase behind the scenes iPhone pics. When users are searching on Houzz, they are trying to gain information on your level of professionalism, project quality, and other business characteristics. They will do their research on your brand further on sites such as Facebook and Instagram if you have made the cut from Houzz. Projects on Houzz are critical because they showcase your expertise. You can optimize each project by using SEO to build your titles, descriptions, and keywords.

- Houzz ideabooks: If you do not have any new imagery and are still looking for a way to keep your Houzz profile looking active, you can utilize ideabooks. These are ways to collaborate or share designs that you like. Simply save an image on Houzz and create an ideabook to include this image under. You can create multiple ideabooks and save images under them in a structure very similar to pinning on related topic boards on Pinterest.

How Often Should You Post on Houzz?

By nature, posting on Houzz is very time-intensive. Projects can take weeks or even months to complete. Staging and sending professional photographers through after the project is complete also adds time to the overall timeline.

Houzz understands the needs of remodelers. Posting on Houzz doesn't need to be daily or even weekly. In fact, while we do recommend posting imagery as soon as a project is complete to better showcase your expertise in a timely manner, monthly posting seems to be the norm. If you don't have projects or photography completed yet and it's almost the end of the month, we recommend creating an ideabook instead to share relevant content that way.

How to Interact on Houzz

Houzz offers three main ways to interact with its users:

- Reviews: Houzz recommends continually asking for reviews. They have made the process even simpler by sending out emails to clients of yours who have Houzz profiles asking specifically if they would like to review you. Reviews are a large element of Houzz's algorithm. But on top of that, reviews are essentially word-of-mouth marketing and therefore carry a lot of weight.

- Questions: Houzz users can ask questions related to your imagery. For example, if a user is searching for Seattle design-build remodelers and comes across your profile and starts sifting through your imagery and stumbles across a beautiful bathroom renovation with a stunning chandelier, that user can submit a question to you asking how they can purchase the same chandelier. Answering questions is good for your Houzz algorithm as well as building your brand as a helpful and reliable source of information.

• Messages: Another way Houzz users can reach out to you is directly through a messaging board. This is most used when asking a local professional if they service a specific area or if they have a question directly related to their future remodeling plans. Responding to messages in a timely manner is another ranking factor for Houzz, so be sure to keep an eye on your inbox or opt for a text or email notification when a message is received.

Advertising and Lead Generation on Houzz

Advertising on Houzz can be pricey, but we have discovered a couple of options to utilize Houzz for lead generation for free.

Project SEO

When building your projects, you are able to write a project description. We recommend linking a related eBook download landing page in that description—if the project is a newly remodeled kitchen, you should link to an eBook about kitchen design trends or a case study on a kitchen renovation. This is the easiest way to draw Houzz users directly to your website.

Pro Plus Accounts

A Houzz Pro Plus account costs about $350 per month per location and per service. In other words, you're looking at a minimum of $4.2K annually to be promoted in Houzz. With a Pro Plus account, you get a few big benefits such as gaining a Houzz rep to help you maximize your profile, showing up more readily in searches based on location, and appearing as the third featured company on the Houzz home page (based on location again). These accounts specifically target a selected city rather than county or zip code breakdown. If you work within several cities, we recommend you select the most lucrative city rather than targeting multiple cities—unless you want to see your bill increase even further.

Sponsored Articles

Houzz offers its writing team to write an article on a recent project you completed to feature in their blog and newsletter. The promotional piece would appear in their Houzz Stories section for a limited amount of time and would also go out in Houzz's newsletter for a hefty bill of over $2K.

Analytics and Problem Solving on Houzz

If your profile isn't performing well, before you give up on Houzz, be sure to check the usual suspects.

Analytics

When logged into your professional profile, you can access basic analytics from the dashboards tab in the top menu. You can discover which images and projects are getting the most views, saves, impressions, and other such information, as well as how many impressions or views your profile has gotten in the past one to three months. If you have a Pro Plus account, this will be broken down by promoted and organic traffic.

Professional Photography

I can't stress enough the need for professional photography. In fact, a Houzz rep once shared privately that pictures that aren't aesthetically pleasing or professional will not show up in searches. They can be detrimental to your brand on Houzz, so invest in a professional photographer. If you feel that your images aren't getting saves and your profile isn't getting views, this could be the reason.

All Other Social Media Platforms

What about Twitter and Pinterest? These platforms have proven not to be imperative lead generators for contractors, remodelers, and builders, so it's that much more important to really focus on Facebook, Instagram, and Houzz.

CHAPTER 6

Fill Your Funnel

CREATE INCREDIBLE CONTENT

In this chapter, I'll show you how to start creating content at scale so that you will start drawing in customers like never before. As you start to build your content machine, you want to be thinking in three main categories: written content, visual content, and audio content.

Today our customers like to consume information. Lots of it. As a society, we're always reading the news and articles, watching videos on social media, and listening to podcasts. The end goal here is that you start to become the media.

If you're going to become the media, you need to start thinking like a publisher. What kind of information does your audience care about? How do they want to consume that information? Where do they want to consume it?

Let's look at an example. Your prospect wants to know about

cost and asks, "How much does it cost to remodel a kitchen in Denver?" Prospects regularly google how much remodeling will cost in their city. Because the internet has pretty much anything anyone wants to know, your prospect starts finding websites and articles that talk about cost.

However, there's a problem. Your prospect is getting this information from other sources. These sources may not be accurate. These sources may be misinforming your prospect. But most importantly, your prospect isn't getting the information from you. This is a missed opportunity to attract prospects to your website and your brand and also a missed opportunity to start building trust and establish your expertise.

You want to be the resource where your prospects get all their information. Education is the new marketing. If your prospects are doing their research on your website and getting all their desired information, you and your company are elevated in their mind.

It's similar to when you go to a conference and listen to a speaker. They automatically have more credibility, so you trust what they say. Your mind automatically goes through a few assumptions that lead to your trust.

1. The event wouldn't have hired a speaker with no credentials.

2. If they are speaking, they must have lots of experience.

3. Most people fear public speaking, so you assume they must be a confident individual if they are speaking.

It's not completely the same when you write content on a blog, but it's very similar. We tend to give a lot of credibility to information we find online. As you build your own confidence and start producing content in the form of a podcast or videos, you'll receive these benefits at an even greater level because your prospects will be able to connect with you at a deeper level.

Now, let's talk about types of content.

WRITTEN CONTENT

The most common forms of written content you can leverage are website pages, blog posts, and social media content. If you're worried about jumping in front of the camera or getting behind the microphone, these can be great channels to improve the power of your website from an SEO perspective as well as start to build some authority and set yourself apart from your competitors.

As I mentioned, answering common questions you hear prospects asking in the sales process is a great place to start with your blog content.

Topic Ideas Based on Prospect Questions

- How much does it cost to remodel my kitchen?
- How long will it take to remodel/build a custom home?
- Can I live in the home during my remodel?
- What does the design process look like?

- What are all the major steps/milestones in the process?
- How do I find a lot for my custom home?
- Should I build new or remodel?
- What are the current design trends?

The list goes on and on. My team has actually developed a list of over 250 blog topics that I've included in the resources section at the end.

As far as website content is concerned, it's important to have a robust website that is still easy to navigate and learn from. Below, I've provided a sample site map (or website navigation) to give you an idea of the core pages you need on your website.

- Home
- Services
  - Kitchen Remodeling
  - Bathroom Remodeling
  - Additions
  - Whole-Home Remodeling
- Process
- Pricing
  - Kitchen Pricing
  - Bathroom Pricing
  - Additions Pricing
  - Whole-Home Pricing

- Portfolio
  - Project 1
  - Project 2
  - Etc.
- About Us
  - Team
  - History
  - Core Values
- Blog
- Contact Us

The website content serves as your opportunity to provide the core information your prospects want to see and learn about. Don't overthink it, but don't skimp here either. Create the pages as if you were visiting them and consuming them. What information would you want to see? What photos?

Blogging

Blogging is one of the most powerful content tools you have in your digital marketing arsenal. It's also extremely underutilized by remodelers. Many remodeling companies do have a blog, but the last post published is often six to twelve months old. In addition, the posts typically don't have much strategy behind them.

You'll see blog posts with titles such as "Renovating to Age in Place." First of all, this title is not compelling at all. Titles should be eye-catching and draw the reader in. In addition, it's not location specific. Finally, it is not effectively targeting a keyword or topic.

Let's break each of these down.

Make Your Blog Titles Compelling

Without a compelling title, your post will fall flat when it's shared on social media or in an email newsletter. In addition, if your post does start to rank on Google, the title is what shows up in the search results. If the title is boring, it's less likely to get clicked on, which ultimately will negatively impact its ranking potential.

How do you write a compelling title? A quick and easy way to do this is to quickly brainstorm about five to ten titles for each blog post. For example, let's say we were writing a blog post about kitchen design trends. Here's what a boring title would look like: "5 Kitchen Design Trends."

Here's what a quick brainstorming session might reveal:

1. 5 Unusual Kitchen Design Trends

2. 5 Kitchen Design Trends to Look for in 2022

3. 5 Sexy Kitchen Design Trends

4. Top 5 Kitchen Design Trends for 2022

5. 5 Shocking Kitchen Design Trends

Do you see how those add more intrigue?

If it were me, I'd probably go with number one or number three from the list above, but it depends on the content of the post as well.

It took me about five minutes to come up with those titles, and I admit I was a little distracted when I made the list. It's well worth the extra time to come up with a super compelling title because this post will be distributed everywhere possible. We want to give it the best chance of success for getting views and ranking in Google.

Blog Posts Should Be Location Specific When Possible

One of the most common mistakes I see in blogging is not making your content location specific. Let's use the kitchen design trends post above as an example. If your business is located in Seattle or Dallas or Denver, you don't want to compete with companies around the country for the same keyword.

We could easily change the title to "5 Unusual Seattle Kitchen Design Trends." Doing so would target our specific location and keep the post from trying to compete nationally. This would improve our chances of ranking in Google for the area we actually want to be found in, but it would also create a more relevant piece of content for the user. If the reader is located in Seattle, she will feel like this post was written specifically for her situation, which is exactly what you want.

Not every post makes sense to localize, but a majority of your posts should be targeting your local area. This is how you can target multiple cities and towns. A lot of remodeling companies we work with service several neighboring cities or towns, so creating blog content that targets each of those cities allows them to rank in Google for all of those cities rather than just their primary location.

Keyword/Topic Focused

Don't let a good blog post go to waste by not having a keyword or topic focus. If you're like me, you're not in the business of writing blogs for fun. Sure, sometimes it can be enjoyable, but the main purpose is to drive traffic, drive leads, and ultimately drive revenue.

Please don't write titles like this: "You've Talked to Your Contractor's References, Now What?" or "Remodeling Survey Says."

The content within these posts might be excellent and super helpful, but that's not the point. The point is that without a keyword-focused title, these posts won't ever be found in Google, which will make all that effort a waste of time.

I want you to write blog posts that your target audience finds in Google. This means you have to write about things that people are actually looking for. When it comes to the topic of remodeling, there are some big-hitter topics we need to address right away:

- Cost and pricing. How much will it cost to remodel my bathroom, kitchen, etc.?
- Timeline. How long will it take to remodel my bathroom, kitchen, etc.?

- Credibility. How do you find a reputable remodeling contractor?

- Design trends/inspiration. What are the latest kitchen design trends?

- Process. What are the steps/how do I accomplish my remodel?

Once you have a topic, you need to talk about what people are really searching for. With "timeline," for example, you want to think about frequently asked questions. These could be questions you hear in the sales process or questions you know people ask. For instance, consumers don't google "remodeling timeline." They search, "How long does it take to remodel a kitchen?" By using the question as your title, you're matching your marketing to the way people actually do research.

This gives you the best chance of being found on Google.

Now that you have your title, you'll want to break it into sections that are easily digestible and help you cover the topic completely. Using the same timeline example, you might create your title and subsections like this:

Title:

How long does it take to remodel a kitchen in Seattle?

Headings:

- Design Phase
- Permitting

- Construction Phase

- Walkthrough/Punch List

- Warranty

Each section can explain what goes into that phase and how long each phase will take. The goal is to give your prospective customer all the information they don't need to feel comfortable. We want them to feel like they don't need to go to any other websites because they feel confident that you provided all the information and that it's accurate.

By creating comprehensive resources, Google starts to see your site as very authoritative on the subject, and you start ranking.

VISUAL CONTENT

Visual content dominates social media as well as much of the internet in general. Did you know that YouTube is the second-largest search engine after Google, with over two billion users? Consumers are searching for answers on YouTube every day, because they would often rather get that answer via video. Video is easier to consume than the written word, which is one of the primary reasons it's such a powerful content tool.

In addition, it's easier to build trust through video. Think about it: If you can see and hear someone explain something to you or speak to you directly, it's easier to trust them than if you're just reading a website page or an email or a letter. Video allows you to speak directly to your prospects at scale. Let's look at some powerful examples of video content.

The process of remodeling can be scary, and there are many unknowns for your prospect as she begins her research. Imagine you created a quick three- to five-minute video explaining the process. You start with her dreams, work your way to budget, design, and through construction. You explain which stages require payments, roughly how long each stage takes, and then close out with your punch list process and warranty information. This puts the prospect at ease. It earns trust.

This type of video works for you in a couple of different ways. It can actually help draw in prospects who are researching the topic of process or timeline. This is where the scale comes in. You don't necessarily have to explain your process to every single prospect who finds your website. You explain it once on video and get the benefit with every prospect who views it.

It's also great follow-up material for any prospects who have called in and gone through a phone prequalification meeting or even the first in-person appointment.

As you know, your prospect usually reaches out to multiple companies, so the way you follow up is critical. You can send a follow-up email with links to a couple of videos explaining topics like your process. This demonstrates your professionalism and allows your prospect to see and hear from you again.

Here are just a few examples of videos you could create that would build trust and separate you from the competition:

- Video testimonials of past clients
- A company history video
- Meet-the-team videos with key team members
- Topic: How much will my remodel cost?
- FAQs compilation (tackle questions like "Can I live in my home during the remodel?" and others you hear in the sales process)
- Project stories from past projects

Video isn't the only visual content you have available to you. We're blessed to be in an industry where photography makes a lot of sense and is relatively easy to get.

Video and photos perform extremely well on social media. That being said, if you're looking to get more attention on social media channels, video must be a part of your content mix. You can do well with photography, but don't rely exclusively on photos. Even taking a set of project photos and turning them into a video slideshow will typically perform better and remove the barrier of actually having to film something.

Releasing a mix of video and photography on your social media channels will outperform written content almost every time. Here are some photo ideas to get your creative juices flowing:

- Team member photos
- Office photos
- Photos of your team in a meeting

- Job site photos
- Before/after photos
- Completed project photos
- Photos of clients with their finished projects

You can also leverage video content in the sales process to set yourself apart from your competition. Here are a few ways to leverage video for sales.

Prequalification

Oftentimes, as consumers are researching, they still want to call and just talk to someone and ask questions. They want to tell you about their project and get some ballpark pricing. They'll have other questions as well. Obviously, I've already addressed with you how you can create this content and make it available on your website, but you will still get calls with the same questions. Not every prospect will see your content.

I recommend setting up a quick video call so that your prospect can show you the area in their home they are looking at remodeling or doing work on. This allows you to get a much better feel for the project, and you can most likely give them a ballpark range based on what you see. The video connection allows you to connect personally with them and forms a deeper connection with you than anyone else they happen to call.

Now, you've done two powerful things for yourself. First, you were able to avoid spending drive time to go out to their home, and you connected on a deeper level, separating you from the competition. We're off to a great start!

Follow-up

There are some great one-to-one video tools out there that allow you to send quick, easy, follow-up video emails. I recommend checking out BombBomb, Loom, or Soapbox to start. After that initial call, send a quick video thank you message. It can be simple: "Hey Mary, thanks for reaching out to us at ABC Remodeling. I enjoyed learning about your project, and I'm looking forward to taking the next step and meeting in person at our office. I've attached a few helpful resources for you to review before we meet. See you soon!"

Again, you're taking a quick extra step to deepen your relationship with your prospect and continue to add value. You can send a simple video email like this one after every interaction or meeting with your prospect.

Delivering Your Service

The customer experience is what leads to you getting more referrals and spurring word of mouth about your business. Here are a few ideas on how you can use video throughout the design and construction process to enhance the customer experience you deliver and help you land more future customers.

- Send a weekly video email update. This can come from anyone on your team—the owner, a project manager, a designer, or even an office manager. Imagine how delighted your customers would be if they received a quick video update from your on-site project manager at the end of the week, letting them know how much progress you made and what to expect the following week.

- Communicate on design work. Your designer could send video updates to your customers with progress made, ideas, and feedback.

- Have quick video calls if you need customer input and they aren't on the job site. Use Zoom or even FaceTime to show your customers something "in person." This saves both of you time and keeps the project moving.

- Explain billing. You could have someone in accounting send a quick video along with a bill, explaining all the details. This helps avoid questions or back-and-forth around a bill.

AUDIO CONTENT

I believe one of the biggest opportunities for remodelers right now is via audio content. Specifically, I think the opportunity is with podcasting. If you're not a regular podcast listener, you're starting to become part of the minority. Podcasting is on the rise in a big way. People want two things with their radio: less ads and more choice. Podcasting gives them both.

Fewer people are listening to the radio because we already have all the music we want on our smartphones. If you like listening to the radio to get your news or you like the entertainment value of the talk shows, you can now get both through various podcasts.

I'm hoping that as you're reading this book, you're seeing a big theme. The way people shop, buy, and consume information is vastly different than the way it used to be when you went to a salesperson for the information. We want access to everything all the time. And we want to access the content we like and enjoy. Podcasting is just capitalizing on this shift. People are moving away from radio for more choice, fewer ads, and more of what they like.

Now you're probably thinking, "As a remodeler, how can I take advantage of podcasting? Isn't that just for big names or influencers?" No. Podcasting is how you'll become the big name and the influencer. Right now, there aren't a lot of good local podcasts. It's mostly just been radio stations creating the same content they broadcast. However, there's a lot of room for a business owner to come in and create an amazing podcast for the town of Amarillo, Texas, or Weston, Vermont, or Laguna Beach, California.

Let's paint the vision here. Let's say you decided to create a podcast called *The Laguna Beach Home Show*. Clever name, I know. This will be a weekly show, and each week you will bring on a different guest and interview them. Here are some potential guests:

1. Architects

2. Real estate agents

3. Remodeling designers

4. Interior designers

5. Home stagers

6. Investors

7. Property managers

8. Appraisers

If you only invited architects to be on the show, and you did only one episode each month, after a year, you'd have twelve new relationships with people who can send you work.

You can also share these podcast recordings with prospects. After someone calls in, you could send a follow-up email before your first meeting and share an episode for them to listen to. This not only adds credibility to you, but they also get to hear you before meeting in person. They'll feel like they already know you. I can't overstate how big of an impact this will have on your sales process.

You could even do solo episodes where you explain your process and discuss the latest design trends or interesting projects you and your team are working on. These can also serve as useful "homework" for prospects. These pieces are great for sharing on social media as well. You'll start to become the go-to source for all remodeling information. Your clients and prospects can share your podcast and help spread the word.

This is just scratching the surface of this opportunity. If you want to build your network of high-net-worth individuals, you could bring on local business owners and interview them about their businesses and help promote them. After some time, you'll have a big network of business owners and people who are interested in listening to those business owners. These are the type of people who will pay for the larger remodeling projects.

This strategy all comes down to adding value to the world first. As you create a show that provides good information, insight, and help to your audience, you'll be the thought leader in the remodeling space in your town. And one of the best parts of all of this? You just have to ask questions. You don't even have to be in the spotlight if that's something that feels scary or uncomfortable.

Another opportunity to set yourself apart with audio is by publishing a book and then creating an audio version of that book. Books add major credibility to you and your company. Think about the process a consumer goes through when deciding which company to go with. They look at price, reviews, and timeline, and they often want references. All the information they seek is in an effort to identify your credibility as a company. Can and will you do what you say you will do at a price and timeline that works for them?

If the consumer is deciding between your company and a competitor, and you've written a book and are a published author, you stand apart. As the consumer listens to your audiobook, you're getting more time with them. They get to hear your voice, your philosophy, your style.

DISTRIBUTE YOUR CONTENT

The biggest mistake I see companies make when it comes to publishing content is failing to distribute that content. Imagine an author publishing a book but not distributing it to bookstores or putting it up for sale on Amazon. It wouldn't reach anyone.

This is the same for your content online. Let's look at your blog as an example. You've just finished an amazing article discussing the cost of a kitchen remodel in your city. You publish it and kick up your feet and wait, but no one sees it.

No one sees it because no one knows it's there. It will take some time for Google to rank this post in their search engine and for people to actually start searching and finding it. Refer to chapter 5 on SEO. How can you get more people to this post quickly?

Well, in the old days, you used to have to pay to create content and then pay for distribution. However, we're living in exciting times. Here's an old model example. You'd pay to create some sort of ad, whether it was for a magazine, newspaper, or TV. You'd need to pay to have someone design it, write the copy, and produce it. After that, you'd need to spend money to actually place it in the magazine or on TV. You'd pay twice.

The new model provides us with free distribution. You still have to pay to create your content (similar to the ad) in either money or time spent, but now you can distribute that content for virtually nothing.

With the blog post mentioned earlier about the cost of remodeling a kitchen, for example, once it's live on your website, the next two steps are to post it to social media and send it out to your entire email list. Those distribution channels are completely free. (Email costs a little if you have a large list.)

Facebook doesn't charge to share articles. Neither does LinkedIn. Have project photos to share with the world? Instagram doesn't charge to post images.

A lot of people get stuck complaining that social media isn't as effective as it used to be or that their organic reach is a lot lower than it used to be, but we have to remember that it is a free distribution channel for our content. A short time ago, we didn't have that luxury.

Let's talk about how you can make the most of these free distribution channels. Social media is one of the best places to promote your content. It's best done in bite-size chunks since people move fast when scrolling through their feeds. In the next section, I'll show you some quick tips for taking content and turning it into bite-size pieces that are great for social media.

REPURPOSE YOUR CONTENT

One of the best ways to create social media content is by repurposing. You don't have to reinvent the wheel for every single post. Let's take a video as an example. We'll pretend you just finished up a five-minute project story video. The video tells the "before" side of the story, shows some of the construction process, and finishes with the "after" and some footage of the homeowners talking about their experience.

Here are some things you can do to get more mileage out of this piece of content.

1. Cut out three sections of the five-minute video that are all thirty to forty-five seconds long.

2. Gather up all the project photos (let's say you have ten photos).

3. Find a photo of the clients in their remodeled kitchen.

4. Create a project summary page on your website with the video segments, the photo gallery, and a write-up of the project details and story.

And now, for the distribution:

1. The full five-minute video can be uploaded to YouTube, Facebook, and IGTV.

2. The three thirty-second clips can all be promoted on Facebook, Instagram, and LinkedIn.

3. The photo of the client can be posted to Facebook, Instagram, and LinkedIn, but remember to always seek permission first before posting someone's photo on any platform.

4. The project photos can be added to Houzz as a project and to Facebook as an album, and then you can spread out the ten photos and post them slowly to Instagram and LinkedIn.

With just this simple repurposing and distribution, you distributed the same content thirty-seven times. And you can link back to the project page on your website in each of the social media posts. In addition, you should email your prospect and customer list and drive them to the project page on your website. Then you have all these channels pointing back to your website.

You'll want to make sure you have some conversion points (chapter 5) set up on your project page because you'll be driving all that traffic back to it.

Even if you don't have a video, and you just have project photos, you can take this same methodology and still be able to distribute your content a couple of dozen times. We often overthink content and get stuck on what to post. Quality is important, but quantity is critical. If you're not posting enough content, it's hard to get noticed. It takes repetition to get the attention of people scrolling. However, once they become familiar with you, they start to look for your content, and they are more likely to stop when they see more content from you.

This all really boils down to capturing attention and then keeping that attention, which is why it's so critical to create content at scale and be consistent.

This strategy gets even more exciting if you can get into long-form content like podcasts or video conversations that last between thirty and sixty minutes.

From here, this is what a breakdown might look like for possible content segments and distribution.

Content assets:

1. Full audio recording

2. Full video recording

3. Five audio clips

4. Five video clips

5. Five quotes from the episode

6. Blog write-up/summary of the episode with the video and audio embedded

You'll have a ton of material to distribute across your platforms.

- On Facebook, you can upload the full video as well as the five video and five audio clips, giving you eleven pieces of content. You can also share the five quotes in addition to sharing the blog write-up.

- On Instagram, you can share the five video and five audio clips as well as the five quotes, which can turn into quote graphics.

- On LinkedIn, you can share the five video and five audio clips as well as the five quotes and the blog write-up.

- On Google My Business, you can share the five video and five audio clips as well as the five quotes and the blog write-up.

- On YouTube, you can upload the full video as well as the five video clips.

That's seventy ways to distribute that one podcast or recording. Again, remember that the distribution is free. You want to maximize that distribution while also saving time actually creating new and unique content. Create content, and then promote it as much as possible.

STAY IN FRONT OF YOUR PROSPECTS

A big part of marketing is playing the long game. I'm assuming you're not planning to remain in business for only another year or two. Let's not treat our marketing and sales pipeline that way.

Yes, generating leads who are ready to buy today is important, but most of the potential market out there is not at that stage. This creates a giant opportunity for companies who understand it and are willing to put some systems in place to earn trust and build credibility over time.

Remember Andrew, who spent six years getting to know my company and me and reading our blog posts and watching our videos? Six years isn't a typical journey, but a year is common. Two years is common. Six months is common. As business owners, we have a tendency to focus on now and forget about the future.

Here's something a little quirky that I do, but it really helps put things in perspective. Let's say it's 8 p.m. in the evening. I'm tired and pretty much done for the day, but there are dishes in the sink. I have a little conversation with myself where I ask the question, "Will Future Spencer be glad I did the dishes now?" The future becomes the present a lot faster than we realize. In general, I try to set up Future Spencer for success. Thinking about things in this context makes building a future pipeline make a lot more sense.

Let's say I talk to thirty leads this month and only five of them are really interested in buying from me now (meaning the next thirty to sixty or so days). Out of the remaining twenty-five, ten are not a good fit, and fifteen are in the middle ground—conversations went well, but there wasn't any urgency, or they explicitly said they weren't ready to move forward. Those fifteen people are now opportunities for Future Spencer.

However, they are only opportunities if I continue to stay in touch with them. If I don't, they will quickly forget about me and our conversation. And when they buy in twelve months, who knows if they will reach back out to me or find another solution.

But here's the magic. Those fifteen leads who are possible future customers this month become 180 leads twelve months from now. Future Spencer, twelve months down the road, now has a ton of opportunity, because he has the five people who are always ready to buy now in addition to a huge percentage of the 180 people who weren't ready in the past but are ready now.

I hope you're starting to see how your pipeline expands dramatically.

How do you effectively stay in touch with 180 prospects or leads at scale? Many times, it doesn't make sense, or you just don't have time to stay in touch with them one on one. This is where the power of email comes into play.

Email is still one of the best ways to actively stay in front of your audience, which includes past customers as well as leads and prospects. A large study cites that email generates $38 in revenue for every $1 spent. There aren't many channels that can boast those types of numbers. Part of the reason is that email is pretty inexpensive compared to other channels. Most email service providers are very affordable, even if you have thousands of prospects and leads. You typically won't pay more than $50–$100 per month with larger lists. This allows you to distribute your message to your audience at a super low cost. However, distribution is only part of the equation.

According to Sales Cycle, 59 percent of respondents say marketing emails influence their purchase decisions.[3] That means well over half of your prospects can be swayed to purchase from you over a competitor if you simply stay in touch with them via email. This is a massive opportunity.

This channel will remain important as your target demographic changes and the millennial generation gets older. Millennials, if they aren't already, will be your primary buyers. The use of email for business communications is preferred by 73 percent of millennials.

What does a good email strategy look like? First, you have to put yourself in the shoes of your prospect. She already gets a lot of emails, so your email needs to provide her with value. If she's researching a remodeling project, she probably doesn't want to get bombarded with sales emails. Instead, send her posts about the latest design trends and how to live for a few months without a kitchen, and before/after photos to inspire her.

This is how you stay in front of your prospects. Add value. Money follows value, so continue to add value to your prospect's journey, and when the time is right, they'll be reaching out to you.

That being said, let's also be strategic about moving prospects down the funnel. After sending several value-driven, top-of-the-funnel emails, try inviting your prospects to a seminar where

---

3   "18 Essential Email Marketing Statistics: 2020 Edition." https://www.salecycle.com/blog/featured-en-us/18-essential-email-marketing-statistics/

you'll be educating them on the remodeling process. This still adds value to them, but hopefully, you'll be able to convert some of your email prospects to in-person prospects.

From here, you can start to develop a more in-depth, one-to-one relationship. Email enables one-to-many relationships (even though it can feel like one to one), so we want to turn as many of those relationships into one-to-one relationships.

Whenever I talk about email, this question always comes up: "How many emails should I send?" The answer is to send as much email as you can without being annoying and as long as you can add value. I'm on some email lists that email me once a day. Yes, every single day. Some of those emails miss the mark, but they provide value more often than not, so I continue to stay on the list and read many of the emails. And those are the people I feel most connected to and trust the most because they are consistently a part of my day, but not in an annoying way.

I know sending an email every single day probably isn't realistic for most companies, so I'd recommend sending a minimum of two emails a month. This may be a stretch for you if you haven't been sending regular emails, but it will be one of the best investments you make in terms of time and money.

What are you going to write in these emails? How will you have enough content to send twenty-four emails every year? Here are some ideas to get you started.

1. Blog posts. Share posts you've written on your website. Craft an email with a little bit of context and a personal note and link to your blog. This is a great, simple way to add value

and make sure you stay in touch with your email list. As an added bonus, you'll drive more traffic to your blog, which can influence how that post is ranking in Google. If you're blogging just once per month, this gives you twelve opportunities to email your prospects and past customers.

2. Project photos. Share a link to newly uploaded project photos on your website. This will showcase the type of work you're doing to your prospects, but it also serves as design inspiration for them. This is dual purpose and a big win for you. Even if you add just one new project to your website each month, that's already half of your emails for the year. Worst-case scenario is you're adding projects quarterly, which gives you four of your twenty-four emails.

3. Video. Have a new video on your website or YouTube channel? Sending an email is a great way to drive views of the video. Typically, video is more engaging than text or photography, so this can be a big credibility builder for you, and you'll get more "face time" with your prospects.

4. Social media discussion. This one is a completely underrated strategy. Normally, I'm all for driving your email traffic right to your website, but let's look at an example of this strategy in action. You create a Facebook post featuring two kitchen styles and ask your followers to pick their favorite and say why. The initial post gets a few responses, so the post starts to reach more people on Facebook. Then, you create an email and ask your email list to weigh in on the discussion, and you link them directly to that discussion. Now, you've got even more engagement, which makes that post reach a lot more prospects on Facebook because that discussion

is hitting the newsfeeds of people who interacted with the post. This can help grow your social following, get you in front of more prospects, and keep your existing audience engaged and aware of you. In total, this is probably a thirty-to sixty-minute investment to create the Facebook post and the email. It's well worth it! You could easily use this strategy four to six times each year.

5. **Premium content.** Anytime you invest the time and energy to create a piece of premium content like a pricing guide, design guide, remodeling checklist, or something similar, you want to let your email list know about it. This is an easy opportunity to provide them with added value by saying something like "Hey PROSPECT NAME, we just released this free guide on our website, and I thought you might be interested in it. Here's a link to the download. Let me know what you think!" Now, you've added value, and you've also tested to see who on your list is engaged and interested in this type of material.

6. **Events.** If you're hosting a webinar or in-person seminar, attending a home show or trade show, let people know about it. Email is a great way to get people signed up to attend your seminar or inform them you'll have a booth at a home show. This is a great example of taking your email list and converting "subscribers" to sales opportunities (in-person conversations). These prospects move down the funnel, and you deepen your relationship with them.

7. **Charity or community involvement.** Obviously, one of the main reasons to do charity work or get involved with helping or supporting the community is purely to give back.

However, it also creates a marketing opportunity or simply a branding opportunity. Let people know what you're up to. You don't need to be flashy about it or brag, but it's a powerful demonstration to your prospects that you're not just in business to make money, that you also care about building up the community and giving back to those in need. This type of email can go a long way for your brand and your reputation.

This is just the tip of the iceberg, but I hope it gets your creative juices flowing. You don't actually have to create new content for email. You can easily direct people to content that already exists on your website or social media.

As we close out this section, I want you to commit to writing two emails per month to your past customers, prospects, and your email database. Do this for at least six months, and I bet you'll have more business coming your way. I've had clients who have closed projects after sending their first email. A past client said, "I'm glad you emailed, I was just thinking about a project. Let's get started."

Remember, email is still one of the best and cheapest methods of taking your message directly to your audience.

BUILD A REPEATABLE SYSTEM AND GROW YOUR BRAND

Digital marketing has a lot of moving parts. At this point, we've covered a lot, and I want to break down what the system actually looks like when you get it up and running.

Here's how it tends to function.

We've got our traffic drivers (ways to get more visitors to your website):

- Website content pages
- Blog posts
- Search engine optimization
- Social media

We have our lead converters:

- Premium content
- Landing pages
- Thank you pages
- Calls to action

We have our lead-nurturing tools:

- Email
- Social media

We have analytics:

- Website analytics
- Lead data
- Customer data

Now, the quantity of all these things will vary, but here's what a sample monthly plan might look like for you as you get started.

- Two blog posts/month
  - Includes SEO/keyword strategy
  - Includes conversion points
- One website content page/month
  - Includes SEO/keyword strategy
  - Includes conversion points
- Social media
  - Three to five Facebook posts/week
  - Three to five Instagram posts/week
  - Three to five LinkedIn posts/week
  - One Google My Business post/week
  - One Houzz project added/month
- One quarterly conversion funnel built
  - Premium content download
  - Landing page
  - Thank you page
  - Success emails
  - Calls to action
  - Email promotions
  - Social media promotions
- Two monthly emails
- One marketing report

Obviously, I don't know your specific situation in terms of how strong your website is, what you're currently doing for digital marketing, how strong your competition is, and many other factors that would potentially change this plan. However, after personally talking to hundreds of remodeling companies over the last few years, I feel this is a great place to start, especially if you're not doing anything or not doing all of these activities.

Most remodelers are dabbling in social media and maybe doing a little blogging or email, but they are missing some critical pieces (e.g., a strong SEO strategy and a full-funnel lead conversion strategy).

BRAND

One of the ways to measure brand growth is through your total reach. Reach is the number of people you can get a message out to. Typically you'd add up your total social media followers on Facebook, Instagram, LinkedIn, YouTube, Houzz, TikTok, etc. Next, you'd add your email list to this number. The total is your current reach. Social media is one of the best ways to grow your reach. By sharing content and having your existing following engage with you, your posts and content extend to their networks. If those people like the content, they start following you too.

In the lead conversion chapter, we talked about how to capture email addresses. Use that strategy for increasing your email database.

Brand growth isn't the only important part of your brand. Your relationship with your current audience is extremely important, and you can deepen that relationship by staying in front of these followers. The more they see your content, see your face, see your company, the more comfortable they get with you. And if you're providing them with a ton of value, they start to like you, and an attachment starts to form.

Time spent with your brand is an important brand metric. This could be time spent reading your blog posts, time spent watching your videos on social media, time spent listening to a podcast of yours, or time spent commenting and interacting with you on social media. The more time your audience spends with you, the better off you are.

As you deepen your relationships, you can build brand ambassadors. These are people who will share your content and help spread the word. They recommend you to friends and family. They support what you're doing. The interesting thing about brand ambassadors is that they don't even have to be customers.

I experienced this firsthand. One day, I was browsing one of the Facebook groups I belong to. As I was scrolling, I noticed a thread where a few members were discussing marketing firms to work with. I saw someone I had talked to in the past. We didn't end up working together because the budget wasn't a fit, but the conversations were all pleasant. He continued to get our blog content, watch our videos, and listen to our podcast. And there he was recommending that other remodelers reach out to me because he thought our content was really helpful.

This can happen to you, but only if you add value to people's lives and you stay top of mind. That's what brand is all about. If you're top of mind, when the topic of remodeling comes up, people won't hesitate to recommend you even if they haven't worked with you because trust has been built through content, and familiarity has been built through repetition. It's a powerful thing!

"I'M WORRIED I'LL GET TOO MANY LEADS."

As I explain many of the lead generation concepts that we've talked about in the book, one of the pieces of pushback I get is "I'm worried I'll get too many leads." Or, said another way: "I'd like to get more leads but only high-quality leads."

Well, doesn't that sound nice?

That's not quite how it works. Most remodelers think of leads as people they get on the phone to talk about their projects. These aren't leads. These are opportunities.

Leads start much higher in the funnel. And if you want more high-quality leads, you're going to need to generate a lot more low-quality leads too.

I want you to think about your typical sales process. Someone calls. You prequalify them on the phone, set an appointment, and then you have a series of meetings until the prospect signs a design agreement and, ultimately, a construction agreement.

How long is that process? Weeks? Months? Most of the time, it's months. It could be two months or it could be over twelve months, depending on the scope of the project and the urgency of the opportunity.

I want you to back this up. That's just the sales process. Think about how long this prospect was dreaming about their project.

How long were they researching it? How long were they googling ideas, browsing Pinterest or Houzz for design trends and inspiration? Usually, it's at least as long as your sales process, if not longer.

As we start to generate more leads, you're going to start capturing many of them while they are in the marketing funnel. You're inserting yourself into their research process. Let's say someone comes to your website as they are researching a kitchen. They aren't ready to talk to you, so they download a piece of premium content. Now they are in your funnel. This lead can feel like an unqualified or low-quality lead because if you call them, they probably won't pick up. Or they might email your company and ask a bunch of questions, but they won't ever want to book a meeting. These types of actions are perceived as low-quality lead actions.

You say, "They don't want to get on the phone, so they must not be serious." But taking that approach results in lost opportunity. Think about the way you shop and buy. When you're in research mode, you don't want to set an official meeting. You just want to get answers and collect data in peace. "Don't bug me, Mr. Salesperson."

If you take the approach of trying to generate as many leads as you possibly can and work to capture them earlier and earlier in the research process, it will feel like you're generating a bunch of low-quality leads who never reach out. However, they are lurking behind the scenes. They are creeping all over your website and social media. And then, all of a sudden, four months later, they will surface and request a meeting.

Why? Because the timing is right. They are ready to move

forward, so they are entering the sales process. You'll never force someone to buy if they aren't ready. It's your mission to be a part of their buying process. Educate them. Help answer their questions. By doing that, you build trust and credibility, and you position yourself as the only company they want to do business with by the time they are ready.

Go out there and generate as many leads as you can while understanding that you'll generate sales opportunities down the road.

And if you're truly experiencing too much in the way of sales meetings and you can't keep up, what a good problem to have. You can do any of the following:

- Raise prices (this will result in better profitability and the same number or fewer projects).

- Use automation to qualify the leads (this allows you to eliminate the lower-quality sales calls through efficient online tools versus your time).

- Lengthen the form on your Contact Us page so that you only get serious people filling it out.

You're either going to have one of two problems: too many leads, or not enough. It's much easier to solve the problem of having too many leads than trying to get more.

Start building that lead-generation system today!

CHAPTER 7

Let's Get Tactical

By now, we've covered all the individual components of digital marketing and how to use marketing to become a thought leader. However, one of the critical parts of marketing is the structure and how all those components work together.

I talk to a lot of remodelers who are physically executing on many of these components, such as blogging, social media, and email marketing, but their results are generally lackluster. In this section, I'm going to walk you through how to build effective campaigns that drive real results. I'll show you some examples from real remodeling companies who have executed and succeeded in building thought leadership and a steady pipeline.

Let's dive in.

CAMPAIGN WALKTHROUGH

All the components we've covered thus far fall into specific categories of the inbound marketing methodology:

1. Drive traffic
2. Convert leads
3. Nurture leads
4. Delight

When you want to drive more traffic to your website, these are the activities that you'll turn to:

1. Blogging and content pages
2. Search engine optimization
3. Social media
4. Paid traffic (Google AdWords, Facebook Ads, etc.)

These activities focus mainly on getting more prospects to visit your website. Once you have people visiting your website, you have the opportunity to convert them into a lead. This is where your lead conversion components come into play:

1. Premium content
2. Calls to action
3. Landing pages

After you've captured a name and an email, it's time to figure out whether that lead is ready to buy now or later. Most leads are ready to buy later, so we'll put them into our lead-nurturing system, which is primarily email. That being said, social media can also play a very powerful role in staying in front of leads.

Finally, after you've closed a customer, you'll focus on delighting them. This takes place in the following areas.

1. The service you provide (organization, communication, timeliness, etc.)

2. Email marketing

3. Personal follow-up

4. Unique surprises

What does this all look like with some structure and specific details? Let's take the topic of kitchen design. If your company does kitchen remodeling, this is a great topic to be found for and be known for. In this example, the goal is to start getting more people to find your website and know you or your company as an expert in kitchen design. Let's break down a sample campaign.

A standard campaign is going to start with a researched-backed topic. This research will come from either keyword research to identify what people are googling, or it will be real customer research, meaning it's information you've uncovered in the sales process talking to actual people. After doing your research, you've discovered that your prospects are interested in kitchen design trends, so you set out to start attracting more prospects looking into this topic.

We're actually going to start this campaign with our premium content or conversion offer. We begin with the conversion offer because that's the primary goal of the campaign. We want to generate leads. The goal is to develop a resource that our prospects will find interesting, compelling, and be willing to trade their personal information for.

After some research, internal discussion, and a final decision, we arrive at the concept of a premium resource titled "2020 Kitchen Design and Trends Guide."

Our research told us that prospects love to think about design, but they often don't know where to start. This guide will help them walk through the process, and it will also show them the current trends.

Now that we have our compelling offer, let's build out our campaign components. Each time we build a piece of premium content like the "2020 Kitchen Design and Trends Guide," we'll also have the following:

1. Landing page: This is the page where we sell the value of the guide and our prospect fills out a form (name, email, etc.) to access the guide.

2. Thank you page: This is the success page where we deliver the guide to the prospect and offer them a chance to take the next step (e.g., book a meeting or call with your company to discuss their project).

3. Calls to action: These are the graphical buttons or links that take your website visitors to the landing page where they can fill out the form.

4. Email promotion: This is our opportunity to let all of your existing prospects, past leads, and even previous customers know that you have a free resource available on your website. We'll send an email to your email database and link directly to the landing page. Anyone who fills out the form is a good person to reach out to and gauge their current interest level in doing a project. You can also just use it as an opportunity to personally connect.

Now that we have our conversion funnel built around the premium content, it's time to drive traffic to the website (and this specific conversion offer). Enter the traffic drivers. First, we'll start with blog content. Typically, we want to have several titles that are tied to the overall topic, which will give us keyword ranking potential. These blog posts will serve multiple purposes. The primary purpose is to rank in search engines for specific questions, topics, or keywords. The second reason we're creating these posts is so that we actually have something of value to share on social media. The third reason is that we are using these posts as fishhooks. Once a reader is on our blog post, they are going to see our call to action for our premium content, which is how we convert the reader into a lead. I recommend creating four to six blog posts that all tie back to your premium content offer.

Aside from blog content, social media is a traffic driver. We can create a variety of social media posts that link back to our blog or directly to the landing page for our premium content. I recommend creating three to five social media posts promoting each blog post and the landing page. This will give us anywhere from fifteen to thirty-five social media posts depending on how many blog posts we created. Now, we've got social media traffic going to our blog posts and website along with the individual posts ranking in Google and starting to pull in visitors.

We can amplify our content by paying to drive traffic. You can leverage Facebook or Instagram to boost your social media posts that link back to your blog content. This will accelerate the number of people visiting the website and drive your traffic numbers up significantly. This is a great strategy to supplement traffic if your website doesn't have much traction. You can also use Google Ads to drive traffic directly to your landing page and drive some immediate lead flow.

Finally, we want to leverage email marketing to drive traffic to our blog posts. I'd recommend at least one email promoting the premium content directly and then one email per blog post. You can space these emails out weekly or every other week. The traffic to the landing page will drive immediate conversions. The traffic from social media and email that goes to the blog content will actually help the blog content improve in ranking, which will, in turn, bring even more traffic.

Traffic is the name of the game, especially early on. If you're not able to get people to your website, you'll never have a chance to convert them. We want them finding your blog posts and your premium content from multiple avenues: Google (search engines), social media, paid channels, and email promotions.

Because we started the campaign with a conversion funnel, you know your website is ready to capture leads as you start driving traffic to it.

At this point, you have the beginning of your marketing

funnel put in place, and you're generating leads more predictably. You are sending traffic to your website via content, SEO, social media, paid traffic, and email. These visitors are taking action and converting by filling out the form on your landing page.

Now, we're entering the middle of the funnel. This is where repetition and brand come into play. We are going to leverage email as our primary lead-nurturing tool to build a relationship with these leads at scale. The objective is to send as much email as you can while still continuing to bring value to your audience. I recommend a twice-per-month cadence to start.

Email allows you to send helpful resources to your prospects and answer their questions before they even ask them. And it allows you to do this in a one-to-many fashion. You can write one email and send it to hundreds or thousands of prospects at the same time. This is critical from an efficiency standpoint because as you build your marketing funnel, the goal is to have as many people as possible swirling around the top and the middle. You don't know when they are going to be ready to start a conversation, so you want to be forming and building that relationship from the very beginning of their research process.

Video and social media also play a powerful role in nurturing a lead and relationship over time. The more times a prospect sees your content, your brand, or your face via video, the more likely they are to feel like they know, like, and trust you. These are critical elements in becoming the company they think of and reach out to when it comes time to move forward with their project.

As we take a step back and look at a campaign, it starts with a conversion funnel around a specific topic, and then we create traffic drivers to send prospects to that conversion point. After that, it's truly a branding and repetition game because you don't know if the prospect is three days away from wanting to start their project or three years away. With that in mind, the goal is to stay in the game. You'll outlast your competition because they might follow up once or twice, but they won't stay consistent for months or years. But now you will.

As you get started thinking about building and executing campaigns, I recommend aiming for quarterly campaigns. Again, here's how that campaign might play out.

In January, you create the piece of premium content, the landing page, the thank you page, and the calls to action. Now, you're got your conversion funnel. In February, you write three blog posts, send two emails, create several social media posts each week, and spend some money on paid advertising to drive traffic to this funnel. In March, you do the same activities you did in February to continue to drive traffic.

As you enter the second quarter, you'll start working on your next conversion funnel, but you'll continue to blog to drive traffic back to the original conversion funnel until the second one is ready.

If you continue at this pace, you'll be executing at every stage of the funnel. You'll be building a steady stream of visitors to your website, capturing more leads, and staying in front of those leads until they are ready to buy. At the end of the first year, you'll also have four lead conversion funnels working for you 24/7.

One of the best parts about your website is that it can be your best salesperson. It doesn't take vacations, it doesn't sleep, and the marketing messaging is extremely consistent.

YOU MUST SPEND ON MARKETING

In some remodeler and builder circles, it's apparently a badge of honor to spend next to nothing on marketing. The argument being made is that the business is built on word of mouth and referrals. The only problem with that is when the economy shifts. Typically, we see a drop in word-of-mouth and referral leads during tough times. It's the companies that have steady marketing programs that thrive during downtimes, and they come out the other side even stronger.

There are other problems with this concept. If you should be allocating an industry standard of 3–6 percent (and closer to 8–12 percent for specialty contractors) toward marketing, but you're really spending 1 percent, you might be thinking you're coming out ahead. "I'm spending less on marketing, so that money drops to the bottom line," you say. Well, if that's true, maybe that's a good thing.

But here's the problem. Most companies that are spending 0–1 percent of revenue on marketing are not actually more profitable, because those extra percentage points are going to other expenses. They aren't charging enough. Or they are spending more in other areas. Maybe overhead is too high. This is a problem. It means that if you're actually spending appropriately on marketing, your profitability will drop. You need to build your business and your numbers around having the proper allocations for all areas (outside expenses, sales and marketing expenses, labor expenses, administrative expenses, etc.).

The other problem is that if you're not spending enough money on marketing, it becomes really tough to grow your business. You can usually get to $1 million or sometimes even

$2 million in sales on word of mouth and referrals, but then you stall out. Or you see big swings in revenue from year to year. Let's say you finally get to $2 million in annual sales. Because you're not spending on marketing, the next year you drop to $1.5 million or even lower.

Marketing creates predictability. It gives you confidence to make new hires, buy new equipment, and actually put the systems in place that free up your time.

Run the numbers from your last couple of years. How much did you spend on marketing? What will you spend this year? Make it work so that you maintain your ideal profitability and cut from other areas if you need to.

TOOLS AND TECHNOLOGY

Just like a good remodeler, a good marketer needs his tools. I wouldn't dare try remodeling my kitchen without the proper tools (hammer, saw, measuring tape, pry bar, safety goggles, screwdrivers, work gloves, boots, power drill, etc.). In marketing, our tools sound a little different, but you still need them.

And it's important that you select the right tools because these tools need to be able to work together and talk to each other. A good example would be having the wrong screwdriver for the screws you purchased. If they don't talk to each other, it might still be possible, but it's going to make it *much*, *much* harder.

What do you need in terms of tools? Here's a list of everything you'll need.

1. Content management system (to power your website)

2. Blogging platform

3. Search engine optimization tools

4. Social media monitoring and publishing tools

5. Email marketing tools

6. Landing page and/or conversion tools

7. Analytics tools

8. Customer relationship management (CRM) tools

You probably have some of these tools already. I'm assuming you've got a content management system, an email tool, and an analytics tool at the very least. Below I'm going to describe each tool, its purpose, and some examples.

Content Management System

A CMS is a platform that allows an individual who doesn't know coding to make changes and updates to a website. These systems have become extremely common over the last decade and use a WYSIWYG (what you see is what you get) editor. Typically, when you make changes, it feels like you're working within a Word document.

The purpose of a CMS is to allow you and your team to make the majority of your own website changes without having to pay a webmaster high hourly fees. It also allows you to make changes on the fly without having to wait for anyone.

Some example content management systems are WordPress, Squarespace, HubSpot, and Wix.

Most likely, you're using WordPress, but you might have a

proprietary CMS that was custom built by your website design firm. Typically, these are not ideal, but that's not always the case. As a general rule, I recommend using something that allows you to make a large number of edits without outside help. I also recommend using a common platform so that you aren't limited to one web designer or one company for making your changes. You'll have lots of options.

Blogging Platform

A blogging platform is similar to a CMS but has a slightly different functionality and purpose. A good platform allows you to create individual articles and organize them into topics. These platforms also use WYSIWYG editors to make it easy for anyone to write articles and add photos.

The purpose of your business blog is to create content that your audience is looking for so that you can attract them to your website, establish credibility, and build trust between your prospect and your brand.

Some blogging platform examples are WordPress, Squarespace, Blogger, HubSpot, and Wix.

Note: A good blogging platform will actually be the same system as your content management system. Ideally, you're not dealing with two separate platforms.

Search Engine Optimization Tools

Search engine optimization tools allow you to do several important things for your business. They allow you to brainstorm various keywords and keyword phrases that your prospects may be searching for on Google or other search engines. They also give you the estimated search volume for those keywords. In other words, they tell you about how many people are searching for "home remodeling services" or "kitchen remodeling contractors." In addition to search volume, these tools should also give you a competition estimate, meaning they should tell you approximately how difficult it will be to rank for those keywords. In general, the more businesses attempting to rank for a keyword, the tougher it will be for you to rank for that same keyword.

SEO tools allow you to make better decisions around where to spend your money, time, and effort in terms of ranking for various keywords and keyword phrases in your content and blogging efforts.

There are several keyword tools out there, some free and some paid. Here are a few of them: MOZ Tools, HubSpot, Ahrefs, Screaming Frog, WordStream, and Raven Tools.

Social Media Monitoring and Publishing Tools

Social media tools give you the power of efficiency. It can be extremely time-consuming to log in to half a dozen social networks, post something, monitor the latest activity, find relevant people to follow, and respond to your followers and fans. Social media tools let you see all your activity in one place and even schedule posts in advance. This can cut your time spent on social media by more than half.

The purpose of these tools is to make it easier to participate in multiple social networks effectively. You can monitor brand mentions, retweets, and engagements. You can also create social media calendars by scheduling out updates and posts for weeks, even months at a time. Social media is important for your remodeling business today for three main reasons (there are many more reasons, but these are the big ones):

1. It allows you to engage with your audience and capture reviews.

2. Social channels can drive traffic to your website.

3. Social signals improve the overall ranking of your website.

Again, with social media tools, you have some free and paid options. Here are a few: Hootsuite, Buffer, SocialOomph, HubSpot, and Sprout Social.

Email Marketing Tools

Your email tool is one of the most essential tools in your toolbox. This tool gives you the ability to communicate with your prospects and customers directly. A good email tool makes it easy for you to add people to your master list and segment prospects into different groupings, and it should automate the unsubscribe process so that you're following the CAN-SPAM Act. You should not be using Outlook or Gmail to mass email your list anymore. That's a big no-no! Your email tool will make it easy to design templates for newsletters as well as create engaging material.

The purpose of your email tool and your email marketing is to create a database filled with warm prospects and contacts that know, like, and trust you and your company. They may not be ready to buy, but they may be ready in three months, nine months, or even twenty-four months. By keeping in regular contact via email, you'll keep your pipeline full.

Here are a few email marketing tools: Mailchimp (free up to two thousand contacts), Constant Contact, iContact, Infusionsoft, and HubSpot (free up to two thousand contacts).

Landing Page Tools

A landing page tool allows you to quickly and easily build pages that are built to do one thing: capture prospect information. Landing pages, also known as conversion pages or squeeze pages, are designed to present something of value to your website visitors in exchange for their contact information. For instance, you might offer a remodeling eBook in exchange for a prospect's name, email, phone, etc.

The key is having something valuable to give to your prospect. Your landing page tool gives you the ability to build a page to help you grow your database of interested prospects. (And now you can use your email tool to stay in touch with them!)

Here are a few landing page tools: Leadpages, Lander, HubSpot, Instapage, and Unbounce.

Analytics Tools

Your analytics tool is critical. If you can't measure what you're doing, you can't improve what you're doing. And some might argue, it's not even worth doing if you can't measure it! Your analytics tool is really just code that sits on the back of your website and tracks information such as website visitors, page views, time spent on your website, bounce rate, and so on. Depending on the tool, you can get access to different information. The purpose of the tool is to give you, the business owner or marketer, the data you need to make informed decisions about your website and online marketing efforts. You want to be able to answer questions such as

- Is my website traffic increasing?
- Are my leads from my website increasing?
- How are my visitors finding me?

There are several analytics tools out there, but here are a few: Google Analytics (This should be a requirement for you. It's free, and it's the standard, even if you run another analytics tool with it.), Crazy Egg, Compete, HubSpot, and KISS Insights.

Customer Relationship Management Tools

Your CRM tool is extremely important in terms of managing and keeping track of contacts, prospects, appointments, and sales activity being performed by the sales team. A good CRM will connect to your website and talk to your other tools so that you aren't exporting leads and importing them into your CRM. Today, it's just too easy to have these systems aligned to be wasting time manually exporting and importing contact information.

Your CRM will help you track appointments, follow-up reminders, and revenue in your pipeline. It will help close the loop on your marketing efforts so that you can see where your best leads and customers come from. In addition to being able to track this kind of information, your CRM also provides accountability. Salespeople can now "show their work" by logging phone calls, emails sent, and appointments.

Here are a few CRM options: Salesforce, improveit 360, MarketSharp, HubSpot, and Infusionsoft.

In all honesty, getting all these tools can be a nightmare, which is why my agency uses HubSpot. They have an all-in-one marketing tool that does all of these things but also connects the data so that you can see everything in one place and you don't have to jump from tool to tool trying to find what you're looking for.

SEMINAR CAMPAIGN

How can you use in-person events to your advantage? A seminar is a fantastic way to educate your target audience, and you get the added benefit of the in-person component to help build trust further. I recommend hosting a seminar two to four times per year. This gives you a great educational opportunity to promote to your email list, on social media, and to your community. Plus, if you record these events on video, you can leverage them as "evergreen" conversion funnels that will work for you 24/7. Here's how the campaign looks.

You create a landing page (registration page) for the seminar that contains the topic, speaker, date, and time. The page has a form where you'll capture leads. Next, you'll promote the landing page via email, social media, and manual outreach through local connections. As a bonus step, you can partner with an architect, designer, or realtor depending on the topic, and they can help promote it as well to increase registrations. Ideally, start promoting your event one month in advance. This gives you time to send three to four email promotions to your list and several social media posts.

Once you have registrations rolling in, I recommend sending three reminder emails to registrants: one week before, one day before, and two hours before the event. This helps increase your attendance rate. With a free event, you'll naturally have a drop off from registrants to attendees, which is completely normal.

At the event, work hard to make everything educational. Make your audience feel welcome. Buy some snacks and drinks too. At the end of the event, make sure to offer a next step, such as a free remodeling consultation or design meeting. You want to move people who are ready to buy down the funnel as much as possible.

COPPER SKY: COST CAMPAIGN

Put yourself in your prospects' shoes. Educating them on the things they want to know about versus what you want to share will always perform the best. For example, one of our clients was a little uncertain about sharing cost information online, but we were seeing that people were really seeking this information out. So we created a campaign around the topic of cost.

Copper Sky Renovations, a reputable design-build remodeling company in the bustling market of Atlanta, came to my agency, Builder Funnel, in early 2017 with one explicit goal: to double their revenue. Our team shortly began to brainstorm how we could make the most significant impact with our content. In early 2018, we created several pieces of content aimed at answering one of the most critical questions in remodeling: How much does this cost?

By focusing on the information stage of the buyer's journey, we were able to provide relevant, tangible information to our target audience. We were also able to reduce friction for our client. By creating content that addresses cost, we were able to proactively provide information to those whose renovation projects may have been outside the typical budget of a renovation at Copper Sky. Cost-related content was then turned into a cost report, a premium content offer that is updated each February to reflect the average price of renovation costs based on the location of our client's service area. The results have been absolutely astonishing.

Prior to working with Builder Funnel, Copper Sky Renovations relied heavily on Google's pay-per-click (PPC) traffic, falling behind in the organic search rankings. Copper Sky wanted to grow their organic traffic and produce higher-quality leads. While traffic was high due to ad spend, Copper Sky Renovations was being found for keywords that were unrelated to their industry; they were wasting large portions of the advertising budget. It was essential to begin reducing reliance on PPC traffic and turn the focus toward growing organic traffic through the inbound marketing methodology. We were then able to identify a topic that was not written about often—if at all—and capitalize on the lack of information for our target audience.

The purpose of the campaign was to increase revenue by increasing qualified leads. By focusing on a tangible question that affects the vast majority of our clients' demographic, we increased leads and traffic, and raised the average conversion rate of the Copper Sky website.

The cost report is updated in February each year, providing annual figures for the audience and higher domain authority by the search engines. In addition to the elements listed below, eBlasts, newsletters, and social media platforms were used to promote the cost report in the attract stage of the inbound marketing funnel.

The campaign began with a series of blog posts, each discussing the average cost of four different remodeling projects: home additions, kitchens, bathrooms, and basements. Because we continuously update the blog posts each year, the URLs of the cost report posts continue to increase in domain authority.

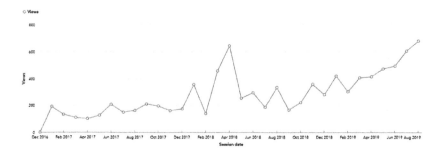

Figure 11: Increased blog views.

Blog views have drastically increased since we began writing about the cost of remodeling in Atlanta, as illustrated in Figure 12.

In addition to a double-digit rise in blog views, the number of organic keywords increased from 116 in June of 2017 to 314 in September of 2019, a significant factor in search engine rankings and website traffic. Amassing nearly 3,400 views, blog posts associated with cost now make up 35 percent of total blog viewership on Copper Sky's design-build remodeling blog.

After successfully publishing the foundational blog articles, we created the *Cost Report*, an eBook that highlights the average cost of various remodeling projects and information about the design-build remodeling process.

The landing page follows standard best practices: removing navigation options, using clear, concise sentences, and quickly explaining why the content is worth downloading. According to IMPACT, the average landing page converts at 2.35 percent.[4] As of July 13, 2020, the Copper Sky landing page converts at 33.62 percent. Figure 12 shows statistics from the landing page (all time).

LANDING PAGE	VIEWS	TOTAL SUBMISSIONS	NEW CONTACTS	VIEW TO SUBMISSION RATE	VIEW TO CONTACT RATE
2019 Home Remodeling Costs Report LP	1,135	425	264	37.44%	23.26%

Figure 12: Landing page statistics.

In addition to the landing page, we implemented a pop-up form on Copper Sky's website. Pop-up forms create a frictionless experience for the user. The user receives compelling content, and Copper Sky receives a conversion (lead). Pop-up forms offer a low barrier of entry to your content and aid in lead conversion rates. As of July 13, 2020, the pop-up form has been viewed 29,653 times by 836 users, and 393 have submitted the form, for a 47.01 percent conversion rate.

---

4   "What is a good average landing page conversion rate in 2020?" https://www.impactplus.com/blog/what-is-a-good-landing-page-conversion-rate

The cost report is a combination of a three-year dedicated campaign focusing on effective landing pages, strategically placed pop-up forms, well-written blog posts, and social media posts. These collective efforts have led to an increase in rankings, brand exposure, and revenue. The overall conversion rate also increased. In total, the cost campaign has influenced a total revenue of $6.4 million.

By the end of 2018, Copper Sky Renovations was named Remodeler of the Year by the Atlanta Real Estate Forum: "Copper Sky has had a strong year to warrant the Remodeler of the Year award. The company increased its digital marketing efforts, which resulted in increased revenue from $2.6 million in 2016 to $3.2 million in 2017 and is currently on track to hit $4.6 million by the end of 2018! Even with the increased volume, Copper Sky was able to increase its gross profit percentage. So, not only did they increase volume, but they were also able to gain efficiencies in production by implementing several industry-leading production processes. In addition to these improvements, Copper Sky is consistently producing high customer service marks from clients!"[5]

- Influenced revenue. When a campaign influences revenue, it means that a lead that turned into a customer interacted with this campaign along their buying journey. Most of the time, this means they filled out a form, but it could also mean they opened and clicked emails or visited specific pages on the website.

5   "Jim Walker of Copper Sky Renovations named Remodeler of the Year." https://www.atlantarealestateforum.com/copper-sky-renovations-named-remodeler-of-the-year/

o 2017 Cost Report: $570,000. When we first launched this campaign, it influenced over a half million in revenue.

o 2018 Cost Report: $2,900,000. After optimizing the campaign, we were able to dramatically improve how much revenue was influenced.

o 2019 Cost Report:[6] $8,714,000. In the third year, we expanded the campaign to double down on things that worked and we added more promotion around it. The site also was stronger and had more traffic coming to it each month.

SESSIONS	NEW CONTACTS (FIRST TOUCH)	INFLUENCED CONTACTS	CLOSED DEALS	INFLUENCED REVENUE
1,488	70	746	28	$6,494,000
/ 1 000	/ 150	/ 500	/ 10	/ 3,000,000

Figure 13: Statistics from HubSpot's Campaign Reporting tool.
The Cost Report has surpassed our initial goals in most areas.

- Website lead conversion rate. This is calculated by taking the number of form submissions and dividing it into your total website traffic and multiplying by 100. Our benchmark is typically 1.5 percent to 2.5 percent conversion for a remodeling website.

  o 2017: 2.1 percent. The website was right in the middle of our benchmark range.

  o 2018: 3.1 percent. In the second year of optimization, we started to break through our typical range.

---

6   As of July 13, 2020.

o 2019: 4.04 percent.[7] After several years, you can see the compounding effect of continuous optimization and improvement. This is a stellar conversion rate, especially with the amount of traffic visiting the website.

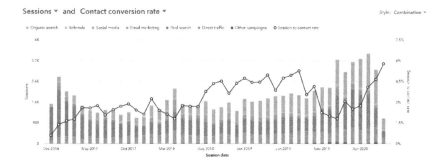

Figure 14: Average conversion rates have increased by double digits since 2017.

Key Findings

- The cost report has been downloaded 783 times.

- The cost report landing page is converting at 33 percent, fourteen times higher than the national average of 2.35 percent.[8]

- The average conversion rate went from 2.16 percent in 2017 to 4.04 percent in 2019, an increase of 112 percent.

- Copper Sky ranks on the first page of Google for over 200 keywords, including "average remodel cost."

---

7   As of July 13, 2020.

8   "What's a Good Conversion Rate? (It's Higher Than You Think)" https://www.wordstream.com/blog/ws/2014/03/17/what-is-a-good-conversion-rate

- Blog posts associated with cost make up 34 percent of total blog viewership.

What Did We Learn?

When marketing a service like design-build remodeling, there are plenty of avenues to explore when it comes to attracting users with your content. However, not all content resonates with your target audience. Through the execution and development of the cost report campaign, we've uncovered that transparency in marketing can yield astronomical results.

When it comes to remodeling your home, cost is a huge factor. Yet cost is rarely mentioned on websites, social profiles, and other digital collateral. By creating a campaign that centers around answering a question often left alone, we were able to raise brand awareness, inform potential clients about their financial obligations in the process, and increase the number of qualified leads.

Since then, the cost report has been implemented with a handful of clients across the country, each successful in their own right.

YOUR WEBSITE AND DIGITAL CONTENT ARE MARKETING ASSETS, NOT AN EXPENSE

One of my favorite parts about digital marketing is that many activities are actually more like assets that compound in value over time versus expenses that you have to continue to pay over and over again to get the same result.

As an example, let's say you decide to take out an ad in a magazine, and the pricing for a full-page ad is $5,000. The magazine charges you $5,000, and they include your ad in the next issue. If they have a circulation of ten thousand people, that is the maximum number of people your ad might reach. Likely, the number is far less because not everyone will flip through the entire magazine, but that's not the point. Let's say out of everyone who sees the ad, some actually stop and look at it, and they happen to be in the market for your services. You might get five or ten leads from the ad, resulting in a customer or two. In my experience speaking with remodelers around the country, this is probably generous, but we'll use it as an example regardless.

If you want to get another customer or two, you need to put in another $5,000 and another ad. Basically, the model is put dollars in and get a similar amount back. If you can figure out marketing channels that produce enough revenue for the expense, you've got a good thing. However, you'll always be playing the game of dollars-in for the same result.

Let's look at the flip side and take blogging as an example. If you put $5,000 into a blogging and SEO effort, you can probably get about ten really great blog posts published on your website. If you were publishing two blog posts each month, you'd have five months of publishing runway.

Once a blog post is published to your website, it can be indexed in Google, where it can be found in search results. Let's say each of your posts is getting five to ten visitors per month, so you're now getting fifty to a hundred visitors per month. However, you don't have to keep paying to have those same blog posts published like you do with the print ads. Every time you put in another $5,000, you get an additional ten blog posts produced.

Let's say you did the $5,000 magazine ad spot quarterly, so you spend $20,000 per year. You get the same number of people to see the ads and the same number of leads.

However, with $20,000 spent on blog posts, you now have forty posts published to your website. Each blog post has the opportunity to be found on Google every single day. As you continue to invest in blog content, your website traffic continues to go up, which starts to compound your investment over time. You can continue to put in the same $20,000 every year, but your results increase, meaning your cost per lead and cost per customer continue to decrease over time.

This is the kind of marketing I love—marketing that acts more like an investment vehicle than an expense.

LEAD NURTURING IS LIKE DATING

Too many salespeople are trying to close too early. Remodeling is a "considered buying" decision. It's not a need, so your prospect generally spends a significant amount of time thinking about her decision. And at the end of the day, she is deciding between moving forward with a project versus not doing the project at all.

Urgency is almost always lower as well. It isn't a scenario where the roof is leaking and she needs it fixed as soon as possible.

Rather than trying to close too early, you want to build a

solid relationship so that if your prospect decides to move forward, you're in the best position to seal the deal.

That first meeting is very much like a first date. Both individuals are trying to get to know each other a little bit and see if there's interest to continue to a second date. On the dating side, you're trying to see if there's any chemistry, common interests, or how easily conversation flows and if there's any physical attraction. On the selling side, you're trying to figure out if this prospect is the type of person you can serve, if they need a project done that you are capable of doing and actually want to do. And she's trying to learn more about you. She wants to make sure you're credible, capable, and a company she can trust to get the job done. On the sales side, this "date" most likely takes place on the phone in the form of a prequalification call.

After a successful first date, both sides agree to a second date. This is typically an in-home appointment. Here, you're getting to know each other better and getting more specific about the goals for the project, possible timelines, and digging deeper to learn more. On the dating side, you're doing similar things. You're asking more questions to learn more about one another. You're exploring the type of people you are and continuing to check for compatibility.

Once the second date is over, we go into the ongoing dating phase. Here, there could be many dates. The timeline between dates varies, and the timeline between the first date and a marriage proposal could be years. On the selling side, this is where most people fall down. Salespeople expect to propose and close the deal after just a couple of dates. Your prospect most likely isn't ready for that. If they are, that's great. However, many are not. This is where the selling dates turn into one-sided dates. You're going to continue to develop a relationship with this person through email. You can continue to stay in touch with your prospect by sending her helpful blog posts on kitchen design trends, tips for making the most of small spaces, home maintenance tips, and more. As she is thinking about her project, she's getting to know you. She also will reply to your occasional email and ask questions. She'll call you and want to talk through a few things.

Eventually, she's ready. She wants to meet in person again, and you have the ring (proposal document) ready. During that meeting, you ask if she's ready to take the next step by signing the contract (getting married). She says yes!

This is a little bit of a cheesy analogy, but I've found it to be extremely true in the way many long-term deals play out. Prospects are going to decide on their own timeline. As salespeople, it's our job to stay present in their lives and continue to add value to their research and decision-making process. It doesn't matter if she wants a quick engagement or a long, drawn-out engagement. You're playing the long game, because if you decide after the first couple of dates that this prospect (project) is a good fit, you're not going anywhere.

Take advantage of email as a marketing and relationship-building tool. It will pay off in spades in the form of many successful client marriages.

NEVER QUIT

Remember Andrew, the remodeler and custom-builder I connected with who disappeared, but then we ended up working together six years later? I shared this story with you for a couple of reasons. The first reason is that you're never going to force someone into making a decision they aren't ready to make. The same goes for a kitchen remodel or building a custom home. If the prospect isn't ready to pull the trigger, they aren't ready. Focus on staying with them through their journey.

The second reason I share this story is because I want you to start playing the long game with prospects. The more prospects you have in your funnel that have been there for a year or two years or more, the more opportunities you're creating for yourself. You'll always have the prospects who are ready to buy today, but when you start stacking up prospects who have been thinking about it for years, your pipeline looks a lot more robust.

CHAPTER 8

A Look into the Future

One of the reasons I'm incredibly bullish on podcasts is that I've seen the positive impact our podcast, Builder Funnel Radio, has had on my business. However, I see so much potential for remodelers with this medium. When you have an audience, you're in the power seat with other brands or potential partners. Let's walk through an example.

Let's say you have a podcast with episodes releasing once per week. You have an audience of a few thousand listeners. These listeners are community members, business owners, doctors, lawyers, and other white-collar professions.

You can actually sell ad sponsorships to other companies in your town that want to get in front of your audience. You know all those companies spending thousands or tens of thousands on radio ads in your town? Those are great candidates to be spending hundreds or thousands per month with you, advertising on your podcast. You'll be getting paid to do your own marketing. This is the power of building an audience. Other people want to pay to get in front of it.

Of course, as you build an audience, you're regularly staying in front of hundreds or thousands of potential buyers. Not all of those people are going to be in the market for remodeling, and the people who are in the market may not be ready to buy today. But that's OK. You're building a massive pipeline of prospects. The best part is that when any of those people get ready to remodel, it's going to be a no-brainer on who to go with. They are going to choose the company and the person they've been listening to for months or years.

The final benefit is that you can use the podcast to build relationships with architects, real estate agents, mortgage brokers, business owners, or other higher-profile community members. This elevates your standing in the community, gets you more exposure, and puts you on their radar as well. Many of these people will be able to give business directly by becoming a customer or referring business to you.

As you continue to build your audience, you can turn the podcast into a media arm of your company that in itself generates a net profit while still producing customers for your core business.

As you're reading this, you may be thinking this is kind of an off-the-wall idea. However, it's happening in other industries already and on very large scales. Some podcasts generate seven figures in revenue annually, and many generate six figures.

This concept is going to happen in our industry, so now is the time to jump in before someone in your market claims the space. Not only is it an excellent way to dominate on the marketing side, it's also a new business model that is treating your marketing like a media company, which means you create a profit center that also sends clients to your main profit center.

If you can't tell, I'm excited for you to jump in and take advantage of this!

CREATE YOUR OWN ORIGINAL SERIES

If you thought the podcast concept was a little far out there, this one might shock you a bit. I want to build on this idea of having a media arm to your company, or even just thinking of yourself as a media company.

By becoming the media, you build the audience. When you have the audience, you have the ability to market yourself to that audience or market others to that audience (via sponsorships).

If you look at the media over the last decade or two, you'll see it's gotten much more fragmented. There used to be only a handful of TV channels and radio stations. Then, those mediums exploded. Today, there are literally thousands of TV channels. Channels have gone more niche rather than being super broad. There are channels for food, channels for home improvement, channels for sports, and even channels for specific sports like basketball or baseball.

As you dive deeper, you'll start to see that this fragmentation hasn't just happened in TV and radio. It's happened with newspapers, which had to go online, and now you see news sites and online publications on just about every topic imaginable.

Like YouTube, podcasts allow us to dive into super specific areas of interest as well. I want to show you how to participate in this but also stand out. You do that by creating your own news—your own channel—and you need to go very specific. Create something that appeals to a very narrow audience. This will allow you to create something the audience truly is interested in.

Enter the original series idea. Imagine you had your own TV show that you published to your website or YouTube channel. The show might be called *The Denver Home Improvement Show*. Each episode could tell the story of you working with a client to solve a problem.

For example, you'd open the show by introducing the client and having them tell the camera what they are trying to accomplish. Next, you'd show your team getting to work on the planning phase. You'd create some drama by showing some of the problems or challenges your team had to overcome. And then you'd close out the show by bringing the client back and getting their reaction. After that, you could summarize and provide some intrigue for the next episode.

As you publish this content, you start to attract Denver-area homeowners. They're interested in the show because they can see other people working through the same problems they have or obtaining the desired features in their home they'd like to have. Soon you will have a large pool of potential customers who are getting to know you and your team by watching you on the show.

And guess what? Because you own the channel and the content, you can run ads for your own company during commercial breaks, and at the end of the show, drive leads directly to your business!

BECOME THE RED BULL OF THE CONSTRUCTION SPACE

Did you know that Red Bull Media House, the marketing division of Red Bull, does about $50 million in annual revenue? Think about that. Their marketing department is producing revenue. This doesn't count the over $6 billion in sales for Red Bull products.

Red Bull understands its target market. Their target market is into things like gaming and extreme sports. Their energy drink products tie into those passions. Gamers stay up late and want or need the extra energy. Skateboarders and snowboarders want to be amped up and live for the thrill of those adrenaline rushes.

Red Bull started creating awesome videos of people doing cool skateboard tricks and wild stunts. They started sponsoring those events. But it's the content that drives the attention and spreads on social media.

Would you watch a commercial for Red Bull if you had the chance to skip it? Of course not! But would you watch a skateboarding highlight reel for three minutes or even thirty minutes if you liked skateboarding? Definitely!

This is the power of content marketing. You're delivering value to your target audience first. Then, value comes back to you in the way of awareness, attention, the sharing of that content, and the purchasing of your products and services.

By focusing their content on entertainment value, they get tons of exposure in those videos. The athletes are wearing their brand, and because the videos are their own, they can include their brand throughout the entire piece of content.

Think back to the last section, where I talked about creating an original series. When you control the media, you get to control when and how your brand gets mentioned. And you have all the attention.

Now, obviously, it doesn't make sense for all of us to actually become the Red Bull of construction, but think about documenting all the work you do. You can create interesting, helpful content that appeals to your target audience. They will want to consume the content. They will want to share that content with their friends and family members. They will see you and your brand more often.

Where do you start with this content? I recommend starting with some frequently asked questions or topics you know your audience is passionate about. The more value driven it is for them, the better off your content will perform. If you make the video a big advertisement, no one will want to watch it.

We all have achieved mastery level at skipping ads: recording and fast-forwarding, muting, or simply running to the kitchen during commercials. So stop creating ads and start creating content. Flip the script on your marketing approach and start to see the awareness and leads increase.

I hope by now you feel more educated around how marketing for remodelers really works today. It's education based, it's value driven, and it pulls leads into your funnel. I encourage you to take this information and put it into action. Start creating marketing people actually like, and you'll start to see your business grow.

You've got the blueprint. Now, it's time to execute!

APPENDIX

EMAIL SCRIPTS/TEMPLATES
Follow-up email to a premium content download:

[[Name]],

Thanks for downloading our [[Insert description of content to be downloaded]]. Remodeling is a big decision, and we want you to be well informed. I hope you find the guide helpful as you're researching your project, and I also wanted to let you know about a few additional resources we have available to you:

- Insert link to blog post
- Insert link to video
- Insert link to blog post #2

As you continue your research, don't hesitate to reply to this email or give me a call on my cell phone (999-999-9999) with any questions you may have.

[[Your name]]

[[Company name]]

[[Company website]]

P.S. If you're ready to discuss your project in detail, go ahead and book an initial consultation by using this link: [[Link to consultation request]].

Second follow-up email to a premium content download:

[[Name]],

I hope you're still enjoying our [[Insert description of content]]. Let me know what type of project you're considering, and I'd be happy to send you some additional resources to aid in your research process.

All the best,

[[Your name]]

[[Company name]]

[[Company website]]

P.S. If you're ready to discuss your project in detail, go ahead and book an initial consultation by using this link: [[Insert description of content]].

Follow-up email to a phone prequalification meeting:

[[Name]],

I enjoyed our conversation earlier today where we discussed your [[Project description]] remodeling project. As we discussed, the next step is to set up an in-person meeting and sign a design agreement if you're ready to get started. I'll send a calendar invite for the date and time we discussed. You'll be meeting with [[Name]]. He's the owner of the company and is excited to meet you.

For more information about our entire design and remodeling process, click here: [[insert link to your process page on your website]].

In addition, based on what you described on the phone, you might want to check out these portfolio pages on our website for more inspiration.

- [[Link to a project page]]
- [[Link to a portfolio page]]
- [[Link to a project page]]

[[Name]] looks forward to meeting you soon. If you have any questions or concerns prior to your meeting, don't hesitate to reply to this email or call me at the office at 999-999-9999.

All the best,

[[Your name]]

[[Company name]]

[[Company website]]

P.S. We just won [[insert any award here]]. You can read more about it here: [[insert link to award write-up or press release]].

BOOK HOMEWORK AND BONUSES

For all Book Homework and Bonuses such as the Buyer Persona Template, Additional Resources on SEO, and 257 Effective Home Builder Blog Topic Ideas visit:

www.RemodelerMarketingBlueprint.com

About the Author

Spencer Powell comes from a long line of builders who have been in the industry for over 110 years, dating back to his great-grandfather. Spencer began his career marketing his uncles' business, where he helped successfully execute the company's shift from only offering home-building services to include a remodeling division during the 2008 housing crash, a pivotal maneuver which helped support new home revenue until demand for building services was renewed. Since then, Spencer has proven his expertise in helping builders, remodelers, and contractors generate leads and close more sales by using the power of their own companies' websites.

As president of Builder Funnel, an inbound marketing agency and Platinum HubSpot Partner in Colorado Springs, Colorado, Spencer revamped his uncles' digital marketing efforts to boost their remodeling division from $2 million to $10 million in annual revenue. Spencer has helped hundreds of companies around the U.S. and Canada build better marketing and sales systems by turning their websites into lead generating machines that work for them 24/7. He holds several digital marketing certifications, including the Inbound Marketing Certification and Inbound Sales Certification.

With education at the core of Builder Funnel, Spencer also writes for their widely followed blog and hosts the popular industry podcast, Builder Funnel Radio, where he interviews industry experts and shares tried and proven marketing, sales, and business strategies. Spencer is also the founder of Builder Funnel Academy, the #1 online digital marketing training platform for remodelers and builders. You can learn more at: www.builderfunnelacademy.com/join.

Outside of helping the construction industry, Spencer loves playing beach volleyball, hiking, weightlifting, spending time with his wife and two boys, and discovering just how many times in a week he can eat at Chipotle.

Made in the USA
Monee, IL
22 January 2021

58429715R00111